MW01148097

# The Gospel According to Acharya S

## D.M. Murdock

Stellar House Publishing
www.StellarHousePublishing.com

ALSO BY D.M. MURDOCK a.k.a. ACHARYA S

*The Christ Conspiracy: The Greatest Story Ever Sold*
*Suns of God: Krishna, Buddha and Christ Unveiled*
*Who Was Jesus? Fingerprints of The Christ*
*Christ in Egypt: The Horus-Jesus Connection*

THE GOSPEL ACCORDING TO ACHARYA S
Copyright © 2009 by D.M. Murdock a.k.a. Acharya S

*Library of Congress Cataloging in Publication Data*
Murdock, D.M./Acharya S
 The Gospel According to Acharya S.
 1. Religion—Philosophy 2. Religion—History
Includes bibliographical references and index
ISBN: 0-9799631-2-5
ISBN13: 978-0-9799631-2-4

Design and layout by D.M. Murdock

Revised August 2009

# Table of Contents

# Table of Contents

# List of Illustrations

## List of Illustrations

---

[1] "Leo Taxil" is the pseudonym of Marie Joseph Gabriel Antoine Jogand-Pagès (1854-1907), who confessed to a hoax in his depictions of gruesome and bogus rituals he alleged were part of French masonry.

# Prologue

"Those who can make you believe absurdities can make you commit atrocities."

Voltaire (1694-1778)

"What is this 'religion'? Why are people interested in it? What good does it do to them? Does it make human life any better? Why are there so many religions? What connection does it have with morality? Is it an essential aspect of human existence or can it be dispensed with? Is it compatible with reason and science? Why is it blamed for being instrumental for most of the conflicts and suffering in human community? A correct understanding of religion only will enable us to get the right answers to these questions."

Acharya Satyakama, "The Need for Correct Understanding of Religion"

Following are a series of essays I composed in the early 1990s that have since been revised, updated and expanded in this volume. These essays consist of philosophical musings and rants, and need not be taken as "gospel truths" that must be defended by vituperation and violence. One of the major points of my work, in fact, is to insist that human beings not be tormented or destroyed because of an ideology, whether political or religious. In view of the ongoing religious strife and carnage, it should be obvious that enslaving or murdering people in the name of God ranks as simply evil.

Yet, for this very reason I would like to impart a sense of cherishment and sacredness for many of the concepts contained in these essays, so that they will be incorporated more fully into reality where they benefit humanity the most. What best serves the freedom of decent and moral human beings *should* be defended against spiritual, psychological, emotional and physical tyranny and enslavement. Here I am attempting to define not only spiritual concepts but also decency and morality to a certain extent. I am also delineating a balance between the believing and nonbelieving worlds, especially conveying where I myself reside intellectually and spiritually. There is nothing here to believe, *per se*, but if a concept suits you, embrace it and own it as you like.

Despite the strides made in the past centuries, in this day and age non-religionists and freethinkers remain under assault from religious fanatics and maniacs who would terrorize and enslave us given the chance—and they continue to attempt to silence us with laws designed to make criminals of us if we object to their archaic, brutal and backward religious doctrines. The global political entity called the United Nations is currently being hijacked by such would-be spiritual enslavers, who want to outlaw "defamation of religion" and to silence critics with  "antiblasphemy laws" straight out of the Dark Ages. For this reason, there is a sense of urgency attached to my work on planet Earth, as I do not wish to see true human civilization fall to these plotters who would subjugate us all—and make no mistake about it, that is their goal, as it has been for many centuries.

In this regard, I do wish readers will take to heart these various freedom-inducing concepts and make sure they are not stamped out by religious tyranny and fascism, by using the same tactics as those employed by the destroyers of free speech and human rights. Claim these liberating and freethought concepts as *your* religious beliefs, and do not allow these spiritual terrorists to blaspheme *your* god and *your* religion, which herein are themselves free speech and human rights. Their religious terrorism and mania—their desire to enthrall you under their spiritual tyranny—represent defamation of *your* religion. Stand up for your liberty, freedom and enlightenment, and do not let these subjugators take them away. There is strength in numbers, and we currently have the numbers to defeat the religious terrorists—let us use them wisely and with all due haste.

Let us also emphasize using *wisdom* because, while we want to inspire people to be passionate in their protection of themselves against tyranny, we ourselves do not want to produce tyrants. In this "Gospel," I hope to impart all of this sentiment and more, and to provoke just such wisdom and passion.

### What is meant by "Gospel?"

The word "gospel" comes from the Greek ευαγγελιον or "evangelion," which means "good message" or "good tidings." The term does not necessarily refer to a narrative about a superhuman savior, as many people believe. Nor did it first come into usage with the advent of Christianity. This word *evangelion*, in fact, appears in the ancient Greek book *The Odyssey*, ascribed to the poet Homer and first composed some nine centuries before the common era.[1] The term ευαγγελιον also appears in the novel *Chaereas and Callirhoe* by Chariton, possibly published in the middle of the 1st century AD/CE, with no apparent Christian influence, demonstrating that the word was still in currency 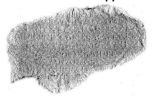 among Greeks at that point.[2] Indeed, just prior to Christ's alleged advent, the birth of Caesar Augustus (63 BCE-14 AD/CE) was recorded in the "Priene calendar inscription" as representing "good news,"

---

[1] Homer, *The Odyssey*, book 14, lines 152 and 166.
[2] Chariton, book 6, chapter 5, section 5, line 3.

using the exact term, *evangelion*.[1] As I relate in *Christ in Egypt: The Horus-Jesus Connection*:

> Scholars such as Drs. [Stanley] Porter and Helmut Koester believe the evangelist Mark, in using the term *evangelion*, was copying this imperial decree and other such usages. Speaking of *evangelion*, when Vespasian arrived at Alexandria, he too was "greeted with this good news (ευαγγέλια)."[2]

Thus, *evangelion* does not belong to Christianity and can be applied to writings such as those you presently hold, which I do believe contain "good news" indeed.

The term "gospel" comes from the Old English "godspell," which combines "good" and "spell." The word "good" in turn derives from the Old English "god," which is precisely the same spelling, of course, as the OE term for "God." There is little doubt that the term "godspell" was viewed not only as a "good spell" but also as a "*god* spell." In any event, for some apparently entrancing reason *evangelion* was eventually translated into English as "good *spell*," rather than "good news" or "good tidings." In this regard, the New Testament tale thus has served as a *spell* that has kept humanity hypnotized for nearly 2,000 years.

The biblical bewitchment and other religious delusions have caused an untold amount of suffering, including the murders of hundreds of millions of people worldwide.[3] With the ongoing mental evolution and spiritual enlightenment of mankind, the spell of organized religion may finally be broken.

---

[1] Porter, 93.
[2] Murdock, 520.
[3] This figure is based on some 250 million murders in the name of Christianity and 270 million murders in the name of Islam. (See Dr. Jamie Glazov's "The Infidel Revolution" for estimates of deaths by Muslims.)

## Armageddon Sick of It!

In addition to the threat of religious enslavement looms the desolation of large portions of the world through religious warfare. The Abrahamic religions—Judaism, Christianity and Islam—represent major sources for the concept of the "end of the world" and "end times," i.e., the Apocalypse and Armageddon. This sick scenario remains a constant  threat on the horizon as blind believers in the organized religions continue to rub elbows with each other in a dangerous clash of civilizations. Those of us who do not engage in such thinking or activities should be completely fed up with being at the mercy of the religiously deranged sociopaths whose intent is to destroy the planet in order to precipitate the "Second Coming" of Jesus, the Mahdi/12th Imam, or whomever.[1] This fallacious thinking and egregious behavior are setting up for the entire world a "self-fulfilling prophecy" that will lead to the destruction of mankind and possibly the earth itself. We simply must recognize this religious psychosis for what it is and move beyond it quickly. This perilous situation represents a major reason for my work in exposing, in the face of tremendous vitriol and hostility, the folly of religious fanaticism.

## An "Atheist" Here to Destroy?

Because of my writings exploring the origins of Christianity as another mythical ideology along the lines of the ancient Greek, Roman and Egyptian religions, and religions in general as essentially manmade, I have been depicted as an "atheist." Firstly,

---

[1] The Mahdi or 12th Imam is the redeemer awaited by Shiite and Sunni Muslims.

the labeling of a person as an "atheist" has occurred frequently in history to those who do not subscribe to the reigning religious ideology, including early Christians who did not follow the Pagan religions. No Christians would describe themselves as "atheists," but Pagans did call them by that moniker. As related by Dr. Jan N. Bremmer, a professor of Religious Studies at the University of Groningen:

> In the first two centuries of our era, atheism had mainly become a label to be used against philosophical opponents but not to be taken too seriously. Even the Jews knew how to play the game and reproached the Egyptians for their atheism....

> The accusation of "atheism" [against Christians] must have been very widespread, since the Christian apologists often did their best to rebut the charge.[1]

Indeed, early Church fathers such as Justin Martyr (100-165) and Athenagoras (c. 133-190) spent much time and spilled much ink attempting to refute this charge of Christian godlessness.[2]

Secondly, I do not describe myself as either an "atheist" or a "theist," because, while I do not believe in the manmade god of the Bible, Koran/Quran or other "sacred text" written by humans, I do choose to perceive a wondrous mystery pervading the cosmos, an immense power that not only drives the sun and produces life on Earth but also creates six-trillion-mile-high clouds of gas that give birth to stars. Because of the dishonesty, bigotry and destructiveness associated with theism, however, I am sympathetic towards those who call themselves atheists, and I

---

[1] Martin, 20-21.
[2] Justin Martyr, *First Apology*, chapter 5 (Roberts, *ANF*, I, 164.); Athenagoras, *Legatio* or *A Plea for the Christians*, chapters 4-25 (Roberts, *ANF*, II, 130ff).

freely engage in atheistic thought where appropriate, such as when some hideous accident, crime or illness befalls a small child or other innocent person or animal. Under such circumstances, it is entirely proper to question whether or not there exists a good god in charge of everything, as taught in religious ideologies. If I must wear a label, let it be "freethinker." Thus, while I may discuss and describe "God," I do not "believe" in God in the typical manner; nor is my description or definition of God meant to be held as dogma. It is merely a suggestion of a perception that spiritually inclined people may wish to consider—take it or leave it as you like.

If you are atheistically prone and do not enjoy discussions or definitions of God or spirituality, you may still wish to read my colorful essays and rants— consider them not as doctrine but as "mystical poetry" addressing some of the most important and profound concepts to face humanity. It is my experience that most people enjoy these mystical or spiritual subjects and that the notion of God will not disappear from the human psyche, so let us at least drag it out of the Stone Age and redefine it.

I should add that there is also much fascinating factual material as I present in my other books but which is unique to *The Gospel*, including a short but succinct discussion of the leaders of Communism and Nazism, and their relationship to religion.

When I first wrote these essays in the early 90s, those who read them thought they were revolutionary— and unpublishable. The publishing industry back then was such that if you did not have a publisher of significance—and there were relatively few—you could expect to sell a handful of copies and to remain obscure and unknown. Writers were at the mercy of overburdened editors and their massive slush piles. Once the internet became fairly popular, however, revolutionary writings such as these found a home, as did eventually also the world of small publishing using print-on-demand. The internet is the great equalizer, as self-published or small publisher books compete side by side with the big-name companies, and a controversial book like this one becomes a feasible project. What you are holding, therefore, is something that would have been difficult if not impossible to create and propagate just a couple of decades ago. In the future, with the push for censorship as concerns criticizing religious cults, such a book may again become nonviable, banned and burned. In this regard, read it while you can, before it is put on the Index of the next Inquisition!

Again, there is a feeling of urgency to my work in

trying to keep the religious tyranny and spiritual enslavement at bay, as millions of religiously deranged and God-obsessed individuals attempt to crush all aspects of true human enlightenment and liberty, covering up and subduing all wonder, beauty and awe. If we do not cherish and hold sacred the freedom-inducing concepts contained in this gospel, we may find ourselves very well staring down the black hole of a new Dark Age. In the end, it is my sincere desire to impart a sense of delight and celebration of life that will act as an antidote to such darkness and dire straits. Please join me in this effort!

D.M. Murdock
aka "Acharya S"
USA
July 2009

# What is God?

"The idea that God is an oversized white male with a flowing beard who sits in the sky and tallies the fall of every sparrow is ludicrous. But if by 'God' one means the set of physical laws that govern the universe, then clearly there is such a God. This God is emotionally unsatisfying... It does not make much sense to pray to the law of gravity."

Dr. Carl Sagan, *U.S. News and World Report* (61)

"The idea of God as the absolute other is a ridiculous idea. There can be no relationship to that which is absolute other."

Joseph Campbell, "The Power of Myth: The First Storytellers"

## God is Now Here
## God is Nowhere

What is God? Is God a giant man who once incarnated as his own son 2,000 years ago through the womb of a Jewish virgin? Certainly not. Is God a man who created everything we see, who speaks to prophets and who writes holy texts? Wrong again. These stories are just perceptions filtered through the limited human mind. They are not ultimate truths. Is God male? No way. This notion is an erroneous interpretation by the male ego.

### "God" is the Life Force

One can think of God as the life force or sentience that permeates the cosmos—gravity or levity, it matters not. As an example of such energy, one can take a plug and stick it into an electrical outlet—this "zapping" is what becoming spiritual is all about. One becomes plugged into "God." But think about that electrical life force: It has no form. In other words, it's not a human being. It has no gender; it's not a male. It has no color; it's not white. It has no size and no container. That life force, or "God," is not a giant man, as we have been told, who can mysteriously incarnate himself through the womb of a virgin of any particular ethnicity. Rather than being historical, these are myths symbolic for the creation of matter out of spirit.

In the Far East, this life force has been termed "the *Tao*." The Tao is the "thing" that makes birds chirp, cats purr and the sap of the trees run. We can also call it "cosmic consciousness." It is simply an energy, sentience or spirit that pervades all living things. Far from having gender, as we have been led to believe, it is the magnetic principle between the male and female potencies. It is also the male and female polarities themselves. This Great Spirit, Tao, or God, encompasses all things. If it is not all encompassing, it is not God. Anything less than the totality is not God. The definition of "God" is omnipresence itself. Nothing is outside of God.

### The Cosmic Mind

The creative/destructive mechanism of this all-encompassing life force can be called the "cosmic mind" or the "universal mind." This cosmic mind projects its thoughts into form; hence, reality could be called "God's Dream." But this dream includes the fragmentation of the Divine into seemingly dense objects and

entities that have a will and independence of their own. As separate entities, we are nonetheless connected atomically to this life force, but the individual ego separates itself into a deluded state. This delusion—or *maya*, as it is called in the East— can become so strong that the creative life force is limited and the entity in which this spark exists no longer knows that it is "God." This delusion, which can also be called "Satan" if personified, is how existence creates, by separating itself out of the whole and presenting the illusion of the many. But this delusion/ego is not anything bad until it is so separate and dense that it no longer sees itself all around but perceives "other," which it is then free to harm if need be or desire arises.

## True Spirituality

True spirituality is defined not by separation but by union, union with the whole, union with the life force, Great Spirit, Tao, or God, that lies behind creation and binds it together. Of course, the separation itself could also be thought of as a spiritual experience, in that it provides an opportunity for an individual soul truly to develop itself. Yet, in that development, we come back to the omnidimensionality of being one with the cosmos. This situation constitutes a paradox, yet one we like to live with, one that we ourselves created, as directors of our own drama. To be separate yet infinite—now, *this* state is "God." Nevertheless, the union too paradoxically represents *ecstasy*, which in Greek means "to stand outside oneself."

Anything that imposes limits on an infinite divinity is not a complete spiritual system or experience. Anything that projects form upon this genderless, raceless, formless and nonhierarchical godliness is not the ultimate truth. The ultimate truth, which is "God," cannot have any form whatsoever, no gender, no race and no hierarchy.

## "God" has No Form or Gender

In the gnostic or esoteric systems of various religions, the Ultimate is perceived as utterly formless. The realization of such formless Ultimate is considered within these systems to be the flowering of consciousness, the maturation of the soul and psyche, the pinnacle of enlightenment. Thus, the definition of "God" as a father-figure in the sky ranks as a lower understanding upon which lies man's puerility and immaturity. Creation has no gender, nor does the creator. "God" is not only father but also mother, grandfather and grandmother, uncle, aunt, cousin, sister and brother, etc. If the "Mother of God" can give birth to "God," she must also be God. Can an imperfect, unholy being give birth to a perfect, divine one? She must also be divine, which makes her God.

In reality, behind the fables, the truth is that the "Mother of God" also has no form but is simply the female aspect of creation, when the neutral spirit-atom begins to divide itself. The principal elements out of the formless creator/ destroyer/balancer are male and female, in equal proportions. The perfect *yin/ yang* balance is the basis of creation. There is no hierarchy in spirit; hence, the female is never in reality lower than the male, as certain religious traditions teach. In humans, the density grows so strong, the ego so potent and intoxicating, that the gender aspect becomes all consuming. One is nearly completely defined by the gender of the material 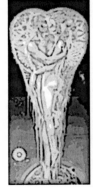 vessel in which the genderless consciousness is carried. While this illusion is remedied spiritually, in this earthly dimension these differences remain between male and female. The remedy is that the consciousness of the individual, through enlightenment or "God-realization," recognizes that it is both male and female and neither. It is an impartial, genderless observer or "witness." Yet, we need not be so hasty in maintaining a genderless state for ourselves, as we are rather fond of the play between polarities, which is in large part why we take birth. Vive la différence!

## The Ego, Consciousness and Enlightenment

The ego will perceive itself as having a gendered experience, but the witness behind the ego is a clean slate of pure sentience. In this dualistic creation, both experiences will happen simultaneously, where one can know the union of existence, the genderlessness and egolessness, and one can *enjoy* the separation. The difference is one of consciousness. The conscious, awakened individual will know in her/his inner being that she/he is "one with creation," but will also know that as the creator of her/his own drama she/he has chosen to incarnate into the denser, more deluded realms, for the sake of the experience itself. He or she has no other reason for incarnating, just as "God," or the universal mind, has no reason for creating except for its own amusement. Once an illuminated soul knows this fact, he or she is free to create his or her own experience and purpose for incarnating. This experience is liberation. It is enlightenment.

Enlightenment, which seems to many to be so nebulous, awesome and scary, is very easy. It is not miracles or magic tricks. Enlightenment is simply the realization of who is pulling the strings of one's puppet. It is the revelation of autonomy to the individual. It is the bestowal of the ultimate god-authority over one's own being. It is when the cosmic creative mind and the individual consciousness merge, when one's mind becomes united with the cosmos. This mental merger goes beyond the mind and penetrates the very cells of the being. This penetration is possible because the god-force resides within the soul-cells of every entity.

**Perceiving the Divine**

There are many practices that can lead to union or reunion with this life force, Great Spirit, Tao, God. We can use yoga or prayer, meditation, chanting or sex. We can play basketball in the Zone. We can eat good food or engage in intelligent, funny or meaningless conversation. We can run up hills, climb mountains and swim seas. Or we can sleep. Ultimately, no practice is needed, when one becomes united with this "godhead," when one has returned to the natural state, from which the human ego has created separation. Reunion with this life force represents the mark of a true religious experience and system. A true religious system is not one that demands slobbering at the feet of a separate god-ego—however large and frightening, whatever race or gender—but one that leads to communion and union with the quality of divinity itself.

## GOD IS BORG—RESISTANCE IS FUTILE

The cosmic union of which we speak is voluntary and not dependent on the grace or force of another. It is not the soul-enslavement prescribed by religious

ideologies that say we must surrender or submit to God. It is merely the experience of totality, of the cosmos. This "coming back to God/ Godhead" is not the BORG experience, wherein we are assimilated against our will to an uncreative group of drones linked to a central mind.[1] Indeed, that totalitarian despot represents the classic description of God provided by

---

[1] "BORG" is a reference to one of the greatest concepts in science fiction, as depicted in the "Star Trek" TV series and movies. The BORG is a collective of drones around a hive mind that travels around the universe assimilating all sentient life against its will. These life forms subsequently become uncreative robots who cannot question the authority of the central mind.

the fervent theists and religionists who will stop at little to suck everyone into their own enslavement.

What we are discussing here is when your individual mind is broadened, such that your narrow perception expands, and you are in another plane altogether, one that contains the plentitude of the void, 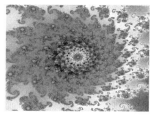 with its infinite worlds—the ultimate paradox and the biggest amusement park. Now, this epiphany or "cosmic orgasm" is God, not the creature that priests portray who wants you to be begging him all the time, while sleepwalking through life. Experiencing this euphoric state actually allows you to be free from the dead GOD/BORG. It allows you to *become* the creator. And from there you come back down to Earth and actually relish the separation, which is also divine, for it allows you, me, us and them to exist—individuals having a vast array of often exquisite experiences. Knowing we are the creators of our own dramas, however, allows us to make those experiences even more exquisite and ecstasy-filled.

# Belief in God

"Truth does not demand belief. Scientists do not join hands every Sunday, singing, 'Yes, gravity is real! I will have faith! I will be strong! I believe in my heart that what goes up, up, up must come down, down, down. Amen!' If they did, we would think they were pretty insecure about it."

Dan Barker, *Losing Faith in Faith* (102)

"Unlike some other gods I could mention, I can actually see the sun. I'm big on that. If I can see something...I don't know—it kind of helps the credibility along, you know?"

George Carlin, "Religion is Bullsh*t"

Contrary to what most people think, belief in God is not virtuous or righteous, nor is it a sign of intelligence or integrity. Mere belief in itself is generally indicative of ignorance and unawareness, despite what religionists and moralists assert. Belief in God does little good at all; in fact, it is the cause of an atrocious percentage of wars and conflicts humanity has fought over the millennia. Nearly every group that has fought in war has believed in a god who was on its particular side. Practically every cult or faction which has won has believed that its god provided it with the win; and each which has lost has thought that its god abandoned it.

As it turns out, to believe that some god person is on your side and opposes your enemy reflects narcissism and egotism. Virtually every side or individual in a contest, debate or conflict believes this conceit, and each is wrong.

## Belief Proves Nothing—Truth Must Be *Known*

A believer's faith in the anthropomorphic god has never made "him" real. The only way believers can make God real to any degree is by killing others or converting them to their own egotistical and ethnocentric, racist and sexist interpretation of God. No matter how hard you may believe in your version of the formless, genderless, raceless divinity, this fervor will not make it so. If such a god were real, there would be no need for belief and faith. Belief is irrelevant and does not *prove* anything.

In reality, the way to make God real is to **know** God, and knowing God will reveal that "he" could not possibly be an old white man sitting on a throne up in a fictitious heaven pretending to rule the universe. This assumption is utterly impossible.

The knowing of "God" comes through a merging of one's individual consciousness with that of universal consciousness, the union of one's own mind with the mind of the "creator." The creator is revealed as being creativity itself. It is simply the quality of creativity, and *not a person*. The "creator" is the aspect of the mind that allows for creativity. It is the mechanism by which the universe creates life and perpetuates itself. The creator has no gender, no form and no race or ethnicity. It is not a human being, as much as humans would wish to make of it. Knowing God as the creative life force behind all creation, instead of a male human being seated in a castle in the clouds, constitutes the ultimate freedom of perspective. It is only in the *knowing*, however, and *not* the believing, that this freedom of perspective comes into being.

In this respect, and because this formless, genderless and raceless truth exists with or without human belief, it is positively useless to believe in God. This life force will have existence everywhere at all times whether or not anyone believes in it. It is like the sun. You do not need to believe in the sun. You can see it and feel it. You are certain that it exists. Even if you did not believe in the sun, it would still exist. It surely does not care if you don't believe in it.

## Belief Causes Turmoil

Blind belief, whether in God or anything else, is not only thoughtless and puerile, it is dangerous, as is evidenced by the countless murders and atrocities committed by believers over the millennia, and by violent acts that will continue to be committed so long as humans think it virtuous  and righteous to believe in an anthropomorphic god who is separate from themselves and everyone else. Such an opinion is not virtuous at all; on the contrary, it is lowly and base, and the mark of the unrealized intellect.

*Belief* in God is a sign not of piety and godliness but of a lack of knowledge and an incomplete realization. No person drowned in belief and delusion can be whole, can be his or her own authority. Any such individual is controllable by outside authority, cannot think for him or herself, and does not move on his or her own authenticity. He or she is not autonomous. He or she is not free. Such a person is not in tune with the force of creation and is therefore not creative. The center of creativity in a blind believer is often clogged up and closed down.

The wise person strives to *know* "God" directly, rather than settling for childish and naive belief in another's interpretation of a formless divinity. And knowing is *science*. Indeed, the definition of science is "to know," from the Latin noun *scientia* and verb *scire*. This attainment of knowledge may be done through study, contemplation, meditation and the ultimate experience of perfect inner silence, and not through any belief whatsoever. There is no giant male god *person* separate and apart from creation who needs your belief or defense. It is not possible to insult or blaspheme that which does not exist; hence, warlike and violent defense of your limited concept of "the divine" is backward and unconscious. In reality, true "blasphemy" represents the treatment of real, living human beings as pathetic, born-in-sin pieces of garbage while exalting an invisible and imaginary giant man in the sky. There is certainly nothing righteous in this behavior. What *is* righteous is perceiving the entire cosmos as sublime and marvelous, and treating decent and innocent creatures with dignity and respect. To conduct such an honest and honorable life, *belief* in God is not necessary at all.

# Praising the Lord

"And now we thank thee, our God, and praise thy glorious name."

1 Chronicles 29:13

"Worthy art thou, our Lord and God,
to receive glory and honor and power,
for thou didst create all things,
and by thy will they existed and were created."

Revelation 4:11

"Praise be to God, Lord of the Universe,
The Compassionate, the Merciful,
Sovereign of the Day of Judgment!
You alone we worship, and to You alone
we turn for help."[1]

Koran/Quran, *The Exordium*

"Praise the Lord! Praise the Lord!" Traditional religion teaches us that there is a God person somewhere "out there" who demands that we constantly praise and give thanks to "him." We must, in order to be worthy inhabitants of "his kingdom," exalt this God fellow in all his glory, which we must consistently mention. In order to be deemed "religious" under the terms of these so-called religions, we must never praise ourselves or bask in our own glory, but we must defer all such compliments and ego-stroking

---

[1] Dawood (2006), xvii.

to "the Almighty," who will reward us for our groveling by giving us lodging in Heaven. The "Lord" needs to be stroked all the time in order for us to secure such a room with a view.

## Is Kissing Arse a Religious Experience?

It is a very strange concept indeed that such an entity as the monotheistic God—who, as an enlightened being, one would suppose is beyond ego and the need to be honored—requires our fawning and adulation. Yet, this pandering is precisely what our "authorities" dictate constitutes a "religious" experience. If we were to apply such obsequious behavior to a human "king of kings" or "lord of lords," we in any self-respecting society would consider this activity to rank as scaredy-cat brown-nosing and arse-kissing. But when this same behavior is done in terms of pacifying an invisible and imaginary deity in the sky, then it is considered excellence.

It is truly a topsy-turvy world when we have to praise unceasingly the being who, according to these same belief systems, shoved us—against our will—into an existence on a planet that these same religionists frequently regard as "purgatory" if not outright hell. How many times have we been told by the same authorities—priests, preachers, ministers, etc.—that we are "born in sin" and must spend our entire lives making up for it, principally by slobbering at the feet of the one who created us in the first place? Should we not, in a sane society, be chastising and rebuking "him" who forced us to be "born in sin" against our will, rather than glorifying him all day long?

## Is God a Megalomaniac?

The idea that the Creator of the Universe and Ruler of the World needs to hear us praising him all the time is positively foolish and childish. Even an awakened human being, so paltry and minuscule when compared to the Great One that these priests have made up, does not need his or her ego continually stroked in this manner. In fact, it is a sign of an enlightened person that he or she does *not* require this kind of praise and worship. While giving and receiving kindness, gratitude and respect should be part of the healthy human experience, only gigantic egotists suffering from deep feelings of insecurity crave this sort of *never-ending* praise; yet, we are told that our presumably self-sufficient Lord needs it all the time or he will throw us into Hell!

## God is a Murderous Tyrant!

Any entity that would punish another being because he or she failed to praise that entity is not a god at all but is a sadistic tyrant who easily could be compared to the most evil of despots, Satan. This supposedly good God likes to pass his days squeezing humanity for praise—or else he'll toss us into eternal hell. This fascist egoist we call "God" is a bully,  coward and insecure sadist who demands constant approval. Then we are told to put our responsibility on this fictitious monster, who flattens cities, murders millions and tortures women.

This concept of a male deity who needs to be exalted, thanked, honored, praised, worshipped, adored, venerated, adulated, extolled, complimented, admired, glorified and idolized is completely out of date and belongs to the Stone Age, when savages were afraid of their own shadows and attributed everything that happened to them to a deranged god creature somewhere in outer space. This kind of thinking does not belong to this era, when humanity must stop putting responsibility for its own messy creation on such an imaginary creature as the male god who sits on a throne in a nebulous heaven.

### God is a Deranged Crackpot

Any being that demands constant praise or else it will hurl its creatures into an eternal inferno is not divine or godly; indeed, it is sick and demented. Anyone who would portray divinity in such a way is also not mentally sound. Clearly, if there were a god with the kind of power that preachers attribute to him, and he needed and/or desired the whining and groveling of such mealy creatures as human beings to feel worthy and good, we should say that he is an egoist of the highest order—yet, this impression is precisely how our religious clerics are presenting God! In fact, if there were such a creature as this God person, it would be highly *insulting* to him to suggest that he has such beggarly needs as in this scenario.

### Enlightened Behavior

Let's get off this warped interpretation of God. God, which is simply Great Spirit, the Tao, the Cosmic Yin/Yang, the Creative Life Force, the Schwartz, or the Big Nothing, has no need for praise of any kind, because *it* is an entity complete unto itself. It is not a human being who feels as if nobody loves it if other human beings don't tell it is loved. No intelligent person is buying this rubbish anymore. No thinking person with any self-esteem is falling upon his or her knees to lick the boots of a giant old man with a white beard who has the power to bestow accommodations in Heaven.

Enlightened people do not see themselves as separate from their own creator. They are the creators of their own dramas. Thus, they do not go around praising any Lord person who they believe is governing their lives. Awakened ones know conclusively that they are running their own lives. Illuminated beings are not separate from the authority that dictates how they live. They are their own authority; they have their autonomy to decide what they will do with their lives. And they praise nothing and everything all at once, because, while they do not grovel before a creator somewhere "out there," separate and apart from creation, they do *choose* to recognize and appreciate the beauty, wonder and awe of creation in its totality.

# Egotists on Earth

"Only the most misguided egotists would claim that they have earned a spot in God's holy heaven as they in their minds stare up at those thrones of God's supreme court."

Pastor Mark Finley, *The Next Superpower: Ancient Prophecies, Global Events, and Your Future* (104)

"Messiahs were abundant, but all of them were egotists who hawked joy-plated creeds through their fading empires."

Rev. Calvin Miller, *The Singer Trilogy: The Mythic Retelling of the New Testament* (163)

"We demand of men a richness and universality we do not find. Great men do not content us.... If they are prophets they are egotists..."

Ralph Waldo Emerson, *Representative Men* (187)

Over the millennia and around the globe, great visionaries have purportedly appeared on Earth to establish extraordinary and universal philosophies that have made an impact upon the human psyche and upon life in general. According to the stories, these distinguished spiritualists have sprung up seemingly from the earth itself, or from the cosmos, with apparently original ideas that inspire thousands and cause these outstanding thinkers to be placed upon pedestals and basically worshipped as gods on

Earth. Many cultures possess legends about certain of their own or some unusual outsider who has seemed to be "anointed" in some way by "the Creator," and who has instituted a presumably new manner in which said Creator is supposedly dictating to "his" creatures.

When one of these creator-inspired visionaries allegedly appears upon the planet there is claimed to be a break from the old philosophies and religions, and the creation of an apparently radical style of living, one that the followers believe is somehow closer to God, as purportedly revealed through the godman.[1] Because these purportedly spiritual individuals appear to be or represent themselves to be closer to God and more worthy of his grace, other people who think themselves less evolved will seek this grace through such "masters" or "prophets." Since the followers believe that there is an anthropomorphic god somewhere "out there," they are open to the concept that he will allow for some of himself to incarnate in and through the various "great ones," who, according to the tales, legends and myths, likewise generally go along with the designation that they are indeed mouthpieces/prophets of God, sons of God, or gods themselves.

The scenario that frequently develops out of such a designation is the virtual worship of the godman/prophet as God on Earth, along with the following of his dictates as the "Will of God." This leads to the establishment of a church, foundation or other such organization to spread the word of the godman throughout the world, with each organization

---

[1] Unfortunately, with the world's enduring caveman sexism very few women—who epitomize truly humane and spiritual qualities such as empathy, compassion and unconditional love—have been considered "prophets of God" or other holy designation over the centuries. This sort of honor upon women has been confined largely to Hinduism, which itself nevertheless is not devoid of sexist attitudes.

claiming that its particular holy man somehow knows with greater surety and insight the mind and will of God. Sometimes the organization surrounding a spiritual leader develops into a cult/religion, where the founder is not only God's representative but also God himself. Therefore, if one is to follow God's will, one must listen completely and with utter submission to the commandments of the godman/prophet, never doubting or questioning his word, and changing one's lifestyle according to the decree of the master.

In finding and obeying such a reputedly godly person, the seeker or religious neophyte may feel relieved that he need no longer worry about whether or not his actions are righteous or just, and whether or not some god person in the sky is then going to be pleased or angered by such actions. Indeed, the seeker who submits to the god on Earth is often relinquishing responsibility for his or her life to the master, who will oversee, whether directly or esoterically, the spiritual and psychological growth and well-being of the acolyte.

## Surrendering to the Master

This "surrender to the master" is common in Eastern countries, where godmen abound. Although many Westerners also submit to a master, i.e., Jesus Christ, people in the West often look aghast at the spiritual practices in Eastern countries. Such believers are smug in their attitude that there has been and will always be only one real master who has ever set foot on this Earth; therefore, they will not ever accept the supposed divinity of anyone else.

This complacent attitude is easy to adopt, because the godman to whom many Westerners submit is an easy taskmaster, being long dead—if ever alive—and unable to make them truly work, as living masters do with their disciples. However, how many Christians— i.e., those who have surrendered to Christ as their master—really live according to the dictates that they presume Jesus mandated? Most "Christians" fail to live up to the standards that Christ purportedly established. Surrendering to a dead master or one who never existed is much easier than submitting to a live one.

This assertion is not to say that anyone should submit to a master in the first place, although the actual meaning of the phrase "surrender to the master" is not as ominous as it sounds or as past "masters" have made it appear. In a pure, spiritual sense, to "surrender to the master" does not refer to giving your power away to a man who is pretending to be God and who will then abuse you in an unkind, egotistical and tyrannical manner. To surrender to the master actually means one admits that someone or something is more advanced in some manner and that one desires to absorb such advancement or excellence. In other words, if we recognize that a bird can sing a birdsong better than we do, and we wish to learn how to emulate a birdsong, we can "surrender" even to a bird in order to learn that bird's talents. Surrendering to a master does not necessarily refer to a man or even a human being, but it can.

When an apprentice to a master of any sort learns the trade and eventually becomes master him or herself, that learning process is also surrendering to the master. In this way, in the true sense of the phrase, to surrender to a master—whether human or otherwise— is to *gain in power*, not to give it away. This beneficial type of submission has been done by many individuals over the millennia. There are people who are so adept at "surrendering" that they become extremely omnidimensional: To wit, they are able to do many things extraordinarily well.

True surrender to a master, then, is a way to learn and to become *empowered*, not to become a slave and disempowered. That last part is the false concept which has come to be associated with submitting to a

master because many people over the centuries who
have claimed to be masters are in actuality grand
egotists who wish to treat others like dogs and have
them serve them. This list of egotists would include
apostles, priests, preachers, ministers, rabbis, imams,
mullahs, prophets, yogis, gurus and the like, who have
determined that they hold the keys to some nebulous
god person and then will dangle them over their flock's
heads in order to control them and gain economic
benefit.

## Many "Masters" are but Egotists

For the most part, surrendering to the master has
gotten a bad name precisely
because of power-hungry egotists
who have set themselves up as
gods on Earth. These individuals
have not had their disciples,
apprentices or followers' best
interests in mind at all; they
have only had their own agendas.
In the world of spirituality, a
true master is interested not in
holding things above his disciples'
heads but in enlightening the
disciple to the ultimate truth so
that the disciple can then become his or her own
master. The definition of a true master is not to
enslave a follower to some rigid dogma or doctrine but
to free the disciple from all outside authority, to allow
the follower to find his or her own autonomy. Hence, a
so-called spiritual leader who exhorts his followers to
obey anyone, whether the leader himself, a father-
figure or giant male god somewhere "out there" in the
sky, is not an enlightened being but a deluded egotist.
No true master has a father figure who dictates what
he or she must do. No genuine master has any parent
and authority of any kind, whether on this earth or in

heaven.[1] A real enlightened master is a person whose authority comes from his or her own realizations, his or her own internal being, which through the enlightenment process has become united with the creative life force that pervades all things.

Any person whose interest is in establishing himself as God on Earth and in acquiring little peons all around who will do his bidding is not a true master or prophet but an egotist. Anyone who thinks he alone knows the true nature of God and then presents this god image as a giant creature that no one else can fathom is not a real enlightened master but a charlatan. True mastery comes when one knows that omnipresent divinity exists all around and is not localized, extending to the smallest creature, which is then to be cherished and respected.

---

[1] This insight is not meant to create disrespect for our *familial* parents—I am all for a close, loving, warm, respectful and compassionate relationship with our mothers and fathers. Nor does it suppose that an enlightened person is wiser or more knowledgeable than his or her parents, merely that he or she is not constrained by parental dictates but is a true adult, in the best sense of the word. This recognition does not represent a call to childish and destructive rebellion, as such behavior would in fact be *unenlightened*. Of course, rejecting detrimental parental biases and prejudices, including religious bigotry, would constitute a *healthy* and *constructive* rebellion.

# Speaking for God

"The Days of God are when Allah, the gracious, the almighty, causes an earthquake. It is when He slaps on the face. It is when He causes a hurricane. He whips this people to become humans... Qur'an says: kill, imprison! Why are you only clinging to the part that talks about mercy? Mercy is against God."[1]

Ayatollah Khomeini, Mohammed's Birthday 1981

"Have you not seen a delusive vision, and uttered a lying divination, whenever you have said, 'Says the Lord,' although I have not spoken?"

Ezekiel 13:7

"Now an intermediary implies more than one; but God is one."

Galatians 3:20

How many times have we heard a loud-mouthed religious leader sputter and howl, "God says this, and God says that?" How many more times do we have to hear that blather until we wake up and realize that nobody speaks for God, not a man dressed in black or in robes waving a book, not a man wearing a turban shouting "Jihad!," not a man of any kind?

## Omnipresence has No Spokespeople

The point is that even to religious fanatics God is supposedly *omnipresent* and, as such, is not, cannot

---

[1] Spencer, 91.

be and never will be contained in one book, no matter how many times the cheerleaders of that book threaten eternal damnation and punishment. If God is omnipresent—a device conveniently used by these selfsame preachers, priests and imams to scare people, e.g., "God is watching you at all times"—then God is contained in *everything*, and that means every book, each person, every animal and rock. *That universality is the definition of omnipresence.* In case the religionists still don't get that fact, let's spell it out:

### "omnipresent : present in all places at all times"
*—Webster's*

Case closed. It is not possible for an omnipresent divinity to be here but not there. It is impossible for an omnipresent deity to be absent from someplace—that fact represents the bottom line. Therefore—paradoxically to the notion that arrogant individuals who pretend to speak for God are misrepresenting themselves—*every* book and *every* individual that claims to be speaking for God must be right, even those which say God is an utterly bogus concept designed to enslave the human race. Since God is omnipresent, God is also speaking when philosopher Bertrand Russell says:

> The whole conception of God is a conception derived from the ancient Oriental despotisms. It is a conception quite unworthy of free men. When you hear people debasing themselves and saying that they are miserable sinners, and all the rest of it, it seems contemptible and not worthy of self-respecting human beings.[1]

Since God is omnipresent, i.e., present in all places at all times, and there is no place that God is not present, then God has also said, through the mouth of Ralph Waldo Emerson:

[1] Russell, B., 23.

> We must get rid of that Christ, we must get rid of
> that Christ.[1]

Or of Thomas Carlyle, who said, "If
I had my way, the world would hear a
pretty stern command—Exit Christ."[2]

Or of Nietzsche, who signed "Anti-
Christ" after his name.[3] His point was
that Christ was a humiliation on
humanity, always turning his cheek
and shepherding us stupid "lost
sheep."

## Disagree, Go to Hell

Those who defend their mythological gods often
reproach such statements by angrily spewing the
familiar, "God says...!" This retort seems to be the only
proper defense the God parrots have, especially that
"God says" those who disagree with such upholders of
the faith are destined to go to Hell. Indeed, if one dares
to disagree with such a self-righteous and egotistical
priest, preacher, bishop, minister or imam, one may be
immediately pronounced as being in league with the
devil and on the way to the fiery abyss for all eternity.
Such is the mentality of the one who pretends to speak
for God.

Those who pretend to speak to the exclusion of
everyone else for an omnipresent God, such as those
who purport that their god wrote a book hundreds or
thousands of years ago (as if he is now illiterate, mute,
dead, disinterested or just plain lazy), are merely
displaying ego deformities of a longstanding nature,
stemming from programming often received as a child.
Those who think that only their narrow minds and
uneducated brains can interpret God—by glomming
onto an outdated and specious "sacred text" that has
been added to, deleted from and forged in many respects—

---

[1] Remsburg, 7.
[2] Remsburg, 7.
[3] Bulhof, 123.

are in reality unbalanced and unenlightened. There is no kind way to put it.

### Everybody Speaks for "God"

The last word is this: If God is omnipresent, whatever God is, then *everybody* speaks for God, and *nobody* speaks for God, in the sense that God is something "out there" to which only preachers, ministers, priests, rabbis and imams hold the key. All those who pretend to speak exclusively for a god that has no location and no fixed point but is everywhere present and occupies all forms imaginable, are either very egotistical or highly unenlightened. The next time somebody shouts, "God says...blah, blah, blah," just remind them equally as loudly and obnoxiously that it is their own ego speaking, not God.

# God's Word

"Our legends and our folk-tales are the sacred lore which you croon to your infants. Our poems have filled your hymnals and your prayerbooks. Our national history has become an indispensable part of the learning of your pastors and priests and scholars. Our kings, our statesmen, our prophets, our warriors your heroes. Our ancient little country is your Holy Land. Our national literature is your Holy Bible. What our people thought and taught has become inextricably woven into your speech and tradition, until no one among you can be called educated who is not familiar with our racial heritage.

"Jewish artisans and Jewish fishermen are your teachers and your saints, with countless statues carved in their image and innumerable cathedrals raised in their memories. A Jewish maiden is your ideal of motherhood and womanhood. A Jewish rebel-prophet is the central figure in your religious worship. We have pulled down your idols, cast aside your racial inheritance, and substituted for them our God and our traditions. No conquest in history can even remotely compare with this clean sweep over you."

Maurice Eli Ravage, *The Century Magazine* (348)

"This Book is not to be doubted...."[1]

Koran 2:1

"He has revealed to you the Book with the Truth, confirming the scriptures which preceded it; for He has already revealed the Torah and the Gospel for

---

[1] Dawood, 1.

the guidance of mankind, and the distinction between right and wrong.

"Those that deny God's revelations shall be sternly punished; God is mighty and capable of revenge...."[1]

Koran 3:2-4

Tell the truth now—isn't it tiresome to hear constantly about how one particular country is the "Holy Land" of God? How a certain ethnic group represents "God's chosen people?" How God had a son through the womb of a "virgin" of a particular ethnic bias? How he raised up a prophet from one specific culture? Must we really hear again how all of God's prophecies and prophets deal with one or another particular nation and its people to the exclusion of all others?

The scriptures that continuously reinforce these types of prejudices represent little more than extremely egocentric and ethnocentric depictions of God and "his Word." Contrary to it being a "spiritual" experience, can there possibly be anything more repulsively biased than a "holy book" that specifically and constantly favors one people over another? What about the bigotry of not associating with unbelievers?

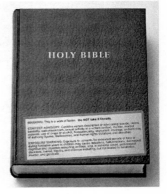

Do we really need to hear about it again, how God gave the land to this group or another, how everything God wants for the universe revolves around what happens in their "Holy Land" and "Holy City" or some other such thing? How praying towards a particular city in a particular manner is a "divine mandate" from *the* God of the cosmos?

---

[1] Dawood, 49.

## Books are Written by MEN

As concerns the most famous of the world's "holy scriptures," the Bible has never been the "Word of God," any more than any other book, since *everything is God.* Like other sacred scriptures beginning in the dawn of human history, the Bible was written by a bunch of men who wanted to make the world revolve around them, their laws, their rules, their ethnocentric and egocentric biases. The Bible is *not* the revelation of any male deity of a particular ethnic persuasion but, among other things, constitutes a *blueprint* that has been followed by rulers and the rich throughout history. It is not surprising that such a document has come to be true now and then. Even a monkey slapping at computer keys will come up with intelligible comments once in a while.

## Superior? Chosen? Arrogant! Conceited!

Of whatever background or ethnicity, people who think that God has chosen them, their land and their laws are living in a dream world of arrogance and conceit. They seem to need a wakeup call to let them know that they are not superior to the rest of humanity. Unfortunately, many people go right along with their pronouncements that God has chosen them. Often even their adversaries subscribe to the notion that their "scriptures" are divinely inspired. But, of course, the competitors then twist these selfsame writings to serve themselves.

It is not one group being chastised here for egotism and arrogance in supposing that "God" or "Allah" has spoken only to them, moved only through them, chosen only them. Any group or individual engaged in this conceit should be under the same fire. In reality, this treatise applies to every religious cult around the world that believes it and only it is special in the eyes of some ethnically prejudiced deity.

Contrary to what religious bigots wish to believe about themselves in order to relieve deep-seated feelings of inferiority, God is not sitting around on a throne watching their every move and granting them the occasional boon. God is not discriminating against all other peoples, whom "he" apparently hates, in order to favor "his" most beloved. There is no such god to be so prejudiced and partial. Indeed, such a creature would definitely not be divine in nature.

So many cultures around the world over the centuries have believed that God wrote their holy books, God spoke to them, God favors them, God loves only them, God protects them against their enemies, etc. It is only by extreme *human* perseverance that a particular version of "spiritual" reality has been forced upon such a large percentage of the world's population.

### Is God a Jewish or Arab Man?

Worldwide, hundreds of millions of people have been led to believe that God is a Jewish or Arab man, because of the origins of scriptures through the minds of Jewish men (Bible) and Arab men (Koran). However, in other parts of the world, "God" is perceived as having a different ethnicity all together and not as a Jewish or Arab man. And an inhabitant of a remote island doesn't even know that the Jewish or Arab god exists.

The idea that God wrote the Bible, Koran or other scripture, spoke only to individuals of a particular ethnicity, admires and rewards them, mated with a woman and had a son of a specific ethnicity, raised up a prophet of a certain culture, is not a reflection of divine revelation at all but of complete and utter ethnic bias and egotism. This fact rates as the naked truth. When humanity comes to this understanding at last, then and only then can we have peace on earth.

## There are No "Chosen" People or "Superior" Races

As long as there are insecure "chosen" fools—of whatever race or ethnicity—running around bragging about how God blesses them over all others, how their country is the Holy Land, or some other such thing, this planet will never be well. All of humanity is "chosen," and the entire universe is the "Holy Land."

Enough is enough. Mankind needs to get over its childish God trip. It is simply the human ego which wishes to assert constantly that God is checking out and rewarding above all any particular individual or group. Humankind needs to drop all such ego identifications as nationalism, racism and religionism, when they become divisive. You are not Jews, not Christians, not Muslims, not Buddhists, not Hindus. You are not black, white, brown, yellow or red. You are not Americans, Israelis, Germans, Arabs or Japanese. You  are simply people, human beings, inhabitants of planet earth.

And remember this fact above all: Your racial or ethnic "history" and "religious" writings are *not* "God's Word."

# On Being Religious

"An ignorant people is generally a religious people, and a religious people nearly always an immoral people."

John E. Remsburg, *Bible Morals*

"Rational arguments don't usually work on religious people. Otherwise there wouldn't *be* religious people."

Hugh Laurie, "House"

People who claim to be religious often aren't. Such individuals believe that following some doctrine, dogma or egotistical self-appointed "agent of God" makes them religious, when in fact following anything, like a brainless sheep, represents the antithesis of true religion. Not being able to think for yourself is not a mark of great religious piety but a sign of being cut off from creativity, which is the realm of the Creator Itself. No person blindly following the uncreative life prescribed by a religious doctrine is close to the Creator but is in reality deadened to the creative life force, which is "God"; hence, he or she is *unreligious*.

## Do Pompous Pride and Religiosity Go Together?

Those who profess to be religious usually do so with great pride and feeling of being good. They think that they are getting brownie points with some deity in the sky or some society creature. Others who hear their declarations of "I am a very religious person" nod their heads in approval, which the sheepish "religious" child desperately wants.

Oddly enough, the pride and ego-boosting that come along with such declarations are signs of irreligiousness, of insecurity and a definite separation from God. By saying that you are religious, you may be implying in effect that there is something about yourself which is superior to the person who does not make such a claim. You are arrogantly setting yourself apart from other human beings simply because you can shamelessly obey the doctrine of institutions that have mindlessly and violently wreaked havoc upon this planet.

## Being a Zombie is Not a Religious Experience

Believing in an invisible, giant father-figure in the sky, and ignorantly and uncreatively following rules set forth hundreds and thousands of years ago by a man or men, rank as anything but religious experiences. The agents of such dead experiences frequently love that so many other people in the world think such stagnation is the definition of religion. They benefit greatly by keeping people enslaved to dead dogma and in a state of  perpetual childhood. Obey! Don't question authority! Marry and reproduce! Don't think for yourselves! Family is good! Father knows best! Follow the Christian ethic! Submit to Allah!

A person in such a state never really knows what he or she is doing, unless it is the most basic of acts, like sleeping, eating or going to the bathroom. But when real, hard decisions come flying down the pike, these individuals cannot think for themselves and must go running to one of their authority figures, such as a priest, preacher, imam or even a psychiatrist, for the answers to their lives' dilemmas. This statement does not suggest that there is no merit in seeking answers and wisdom from others who are trustworthy and knowledgeable. Humans certainly *should* develop healthy social bonds with others and ask for help. Yet, the need does suppose that other people know who you are more than you do and can determine your life better than you can, which may not be a serious problem. However, not knowing yourself and putting your life in the hands of others, whether a terrestrial father or the Great Daddy in the Sky, most definitely does not rate as a *religious experience* by any enlightened definition.

In fact, not knowing yourself represents *unenlightenment*, which is considered the opposite of a religious experience in many cultures and religious traditions. Even the writer of the biblical text of Galatians (4:19) invokes his followers as, "My little children, with whom I am again in travail *until the Christ be formed in you*." (Emphasis added.) What this remark clearly means is that until you *become* Christ—"Christ" being a spiritual state of union with divinity, not a Jewish man—you are still a child, not a completed

adult. The whole point of real religion is to create enlightened, awakened, fully formed adults who take responsibility for themselves and do not pass it off on any savior, messiah or father god. A religion that causes one to become crippled, self-mortifying and self-deprecating is *not* a religion but a social system of controlling the masses through psychological deformation and retardation.

Surrendering your existence to a fictitious daddy in heaven, his savior son or one true prophet does not constitute a religious experience. For those who know what a religious experience truly is—an epiphany whereby the entire universe becomes a blessing— followers of organized religion who proudly proclaim they are "religious" appear irritating and foolish. Get a clue about the nature of God other than what some ridiculous, outdated, biased, sexist, racist and spurious "sacred text" and its cheerleaders dictate. Meditate and feel your inner silence. Then you will truly be able to claim you are religious, but not while you are unthinkingly following someone or something simply because you believe that will earn you marks in the Maker's "Book of Life." Many serial killers and mass murderers have also claimed to be very religious people. Obviously, this claim in itself does not mark a good character. It is not an impressive thing to those who know true religion, which has no dogma, no doctrine, no anthropomorphic god, no saviors, prophets or priests, but simply benevolence, divine love, cosmic consciousness and common decency.

# On a Wing and a Prayer

**"God, protect me from your followers."**

"People pray to God so he won't crush them like bugs."

Hugh Laurie, "House"

"Hands that help are far better than lips that pray."

Colonel Robert G. Ingersoll, *The Works of Robert G. Ingersoll* (IV, 418)

"Love is the very essence of prayer. Those who pray without love, their prayer remains formal. It is an empty gesture with no meaning, no significance. They can go on praying for lives together—no transformation is going to happen through their prayer. They are deceiving themselves and nobody else."

Osho, *The Golden Wind* (1)

Many people pray in times of distress and discomfort. Others do it out of a sense of obligation that some god person is watching them and waiting for their begging and praise. While prayer may have its place, the simple fact is that we are not born into this world to be beggars and naggers. We are born into this world to become buddhas and christs who command godly energy, rather than whimpering and whining to some unknown and imaginary agency in the sky.

## Is Begging a Religious Experience?

Although it may not be an accurate and humane representation, in many places begging is viewed as a disgrace, a reduction in self-esteem, a sign of poor self-image. Yet, when it comes to soliciting favors and blessings from a deity, begging is considered a great virtue. If a person comes up to another on the street and says, "Please give me some money—I am so hungry," some people cop an attitude towards that person that he or she is "less than," even while they might give him or her some money. Others are so scornful they would not even consider giving the "bum" anything.

But if someone looks towards the heavens or closes his or her eyes and begs instead to an invisible entity that some call "God," saying, "Father, give me some money— I am so hungry," *that* begging  is viewed as being highly virtuous and righteous. Our religious authorities such as priests, rabbis, ministers and imams really approve of *that* kind of begging.

The begging called prayer is no less dishonorable in terms of revealing a lack of self-worth and power than the begging often called panhandling. As practiced by many people, the begging called prayer could be viewed to be as pitiful and degrading as is bumming on the street. But this fact cannot be seen by these same individuals because they have been conditioned to believe that there is some god person on the other end of their begging and nagging who is pleased by it.

### Does God Like Begging?

If any such god person were real who enjoyed such lowly behavior as constant begging and nagging, and who also got a real ego kick out of humans praising and exalting "his" name, such an one should surely be considered a tyrant and conceited creep. This kind of personality is intolerable to us from other human beings—we call it a coward, bully or egotist—but from our God, we expect it and go along with it, a behavior truly hypocritical.

Whenever a person arises on this earth who has such a conceited and supercilious "god" personality, he soon develops many enemies who wish to destroy him because of his hubris and arrogance. But this same kind of behavior from our deity is a given, and humans seem perversely to admire that idea.

### We are Buddhas, Not Beggars

On the opposite side of a beggar is a buddha, who

does not ask for favors from any god person but who *demands* that life improve around him or her. In actuality, there is nothing particularly wrong with addressing an unseen entity or entities, and even asking questions of what seems to be nothing. In addition, by focusing our minds in prayer or meditation, we appear to be able to bring about healing by helping to increase the healing chemicals in our bodies. But giving away through sniveling and groveling one's power over one's own life is not the experience of a completed consciousness. To assume that there is some outside authority who has control over your life constitutes surrendering your autonomy. This surrender supposes that someone else is living your life for you. You are not really living your own life. This lack of autonomy represents the problem with having a daddy figure in the sky from whom you must continuously beg favors.

The paradox is that there *seem to be* elements "out there"—one could call them "energy currents" or "powers that be"—which people have attempted to utilize, even ask, to aid them in changing their circumstances. For example, shamans and masters who allegedly know how to speak to such elements or spirits seemingly have been able change the weather, among other purported supernatural accomplishments. They supposedly do this extraordinary act by petitioning or commanding elements, spirits or the "Great Spirit." But there is an entirely different attitude here, one of being in control of the creative life force, of respecting the elements, while not being a victim or patsy of them. Naturally, skeptics claim these individuals are in reality doing no such thing at all and that proof of such elemental manipulation is nowhere to be found.

## Oh Lord, Won't You Buy Me a Mercedes Benz?

Since we are not interested in mind control, we *can* meditate and commune with the elements, *if we so choose*, whether or not we wish to call them God, gods, angels, buddhas, etc. There is no law against what you can do with your consciousness. But keep in mind that prayer is not all that it is cracked up to be—think about it, how many of your "prayers" have really been answered? This insight is not to say that at times prayers have not been "answered" randomly, but far too many have gone unanswered for this exercise to be reliable. As the late great comedian George Carlin remarked:

> So I've been praying to Joe [Pesci] for about a year now. And I noticed something. I noticed that all the prayers I used to offer to God and all the prayers I

now offer to Joe Pesci are being answered at about the same 50% rate. Half the time I get what I want, half the time I don't. Same as God, 50-50. Same as the four-leaf clover and the horseshoe, the wishing well and the rabbit's foot, same as the Mojo Man, same as the Voodoo Lady who tells you your fortune by squeezing the goat's testicles—it's all the same: 50-50. So just pick your superstition, sit back, make a wish, and enjoy yourself.

Moreover, while fervent believers bleat and wail about "witchcraft," à la "Harry Potter" for example, the typical prayer represents mere voodoo and witchcraft itself, as the person praying is attempting to affect supernaturally some aspect of life, whether it be a global concern or a personal worry, such as the status of an "unsaved" loved one. In other words, the Christian who fervently prays for the soul of another, haughtily believing that he or she is "saved" and superior to the subject of the prayer, and therefore has a direct pipeline to the "right" God, is little different from the Pagan or the Wiccan, despite fallacious claims otherwise, except that the intent of the modern Pagan or Wiccan seldom seems to be one of conceit and arrogance.

Curiosity requires us to ask what Muslims are  praying for five times a day? World peace? Global domination? To top the next guy over in a business deal? What kind of God needs this sort of prayer several times daily? If God is omniscient, "he" already knows what we want and need. Praying to him becomes an exercise in futility, in essence a very potent form of mind control. If God were real and omniscient, this pesky behavior could be deemed obnoxious and disrespectful, unless this god is a giant sadist and egotist in need of constant exaltation, praise, groveling and so on. In that case, however, such a creature could not possibly be considered God. The bottom line, then, is that prayer for the sake of pleasing a god several times a day is completely unnecessary and useless. Indeed, a case could be made that such prayer is insulting and disrespectful to God, presuming he needs it for either egotistical purposes or because he is in reality not omniscient and therefore does not already know what we need. Under such circumstances, prayer would be ungodly and unholy, especially several times a day.

## What is "True Prayer?"

Rather than begging, "true prayer" is an invitation to the universe, a welcoming, a jubilation. The prayerful attitude is one of joy and delight. When one is in "true prayer," one has no designation or label; in other words, one is not a Christian, Hindu, Buddhist, Muslim or Jew. One is not mindlessly repeating rote or parroting scriptures—this robotic behavior is the opposite of true prayer. True prayer represents a state of being one with the Absolute. Hence, there is no object or subject. There is only the One.

This experience of empowerment can be called enlightenment, which is what most people should be praying for above all. As an Indian sage once said:

> Prayer is wonder, reverence. Prayer is receptivity for the miracle that surrounds you. Prayer is surrender to beauty, to the grandeur, to this fantastic experience. Prayer is a non-argumentative dialogue with existence. It is not a discussion... it is a love-dialogue. You don't argue... you simply whisper sweet nothings.[1]

---

[1] Osho, *DM*, 151.

How do we attain to such a state of peacefulness? Life is full of treachery and danger—can we not get assistance in changing it? Is there no higher power upon which we can rely at all? Are we simply alone to our own devices, which may be useless? Is this reality all there is? These last sentiments are frightening to many people, which is why they want to believe so strongly in God. To think that they are ABSOLUTELY ALONE on this planet can be horrifying, and such fear is frequently justified, because this world is so chaotic and crazed. We cannot attain to peace within ourselves unless we also bring it about *without* ourselves. Think about that double-entendre: You are one with the cosmos; thus, everything is you, but you lose yourself at the same time. The search for peace must include not only your inner being but also your surroundings as well. And in that search, the "you" becomes more expanded, to the point of being nothing yet encompassing everything.

## Is God a Sadist?

There *does exist* power in the universe. The question remains how we can tap into it. Is this higher energy a person with its own mind and plan of whom we need to ask permission to live in a happy, stressfree manner, which is really what people are praying for? People just want to be happy, without the heart-rending stress and tragedy that too frequently befalls them. Many folks are not asking for very much at all—to live unharrassed in simple enjoyment. One would think that were there a higher power, it could at least bestow that small thing, since it supposedly created us in the first place! What kind of cruel creator cannot even allow that simple reality? This situation represents the paradox of having a personal creator separate and apart from creation who exclusively holds the keys to creation and is the only one who knows the plan! And how come this supposedly all-knowing God doesn't already know what we require, such that we need to ask? Why do a "Jesus" or "Mary" need to appear to tell people how to pray to them, when they obviously know what the people's requirements are, since they are telling them how to pray to get their needs fulfilled?

The reality of the situation is that there is no separation between us and the Creator. We are the creators of our own drama, and as long as we insist that someone else is, nothing will change on this planet. The same dementia, neuroses and psychoses that cause us so much grief, from which we *pray* for release, will continue to rule the mass human psyche. These mental and emotional debilitations are created by the very notion that we are separate from God. According to this belief, there is this immense and magnificent otherworldly being who deserves high praise indeed, but we ourselves—his children—are simply awful, wretched, sinful creatures who need constant chastisement and repentance.

How do we change ourselves and the world? By recognizing that the dense separation between us and the rest of creation is artificial, such that instead of begging cosmic energy, we can draw it into ourselves

and spread it out into the world. By knowing that we are godly beings, not wretches, we can reach a state of responsibility and maturity. And we can get righteously indignant and demand change, instead of begging for it.

In order to have a mature spiritual experience, merely know that there is a difference between a buddha and a beggar. Understand that a buddha *is* God, his or her experience is not separate from any god entity, while a beggar has a layer of separation in his or her perception that God is an entity "absolutely other," outside of him or herself and separate. This separation from God is placed as a "meme" or mental conditioning by the very priests who then profess to teach someone how to pray to that God. Without the separation, the prayer becomes unnecessary, as one is already in prayer with God. One is in fact praying to oneself. As British actor Sir Peter O'Toole says in "The Ruling Class," when asked, "How do you know you're God?"—

**"Simple. When I pray to him, I find I'm speaking to myself."**

And one is then also answering one's own prayers.

# Born in Sin?

"For as in Adam all die, even so in Christ shall all be made alive."

1 Corinthians 15:22

"For all have sinned, and come short of the glory of God; Being justified freely by his grace through the redemption that is in Christ Jesus: Whom God hath set forth [to be] a propitiation through faith in his blood, to declare his righteousness for the remission of sins that are past, through the forbearance of God ..."

Romans 3:23-25

"Original sin may be taken to mean: (1) the sin that Adam committed; (2) a consequence of this first sin, the hereditary stain with which we are born on account of our origin or descent from Adam."

*Catholic Encyclopedia*, "Original Sin" (XI, 312)

One of the major tenets of the Christian faith is that we are all "born in sin," essentially meaning that humans are imperfect wretches who can only be redeemed through the grace of God via his son, Jesus Christ. This belief is founded upon the Old Testament tale of the first couple, Adam and Eve, in the biblical book of Genesis. The "original sin" of which we are all guilty, according to Christianity, emanates from the act of Adam and Eve eating from the tree of knowledge of good and evil, and then discovering their nakedness, after which they were thrown out of the paradisiacal

Garden of Eden, ostensibly for "disobedience." These alleged transgressions through no fault of our supposed primogenitors constitute the basis of practically the entire purpose of Christianity: To wit, redemption through the sacrifice of Jesus Christ, whose bloody death removes our sins. Obviously, the fact that this gruesome act represents an old scapegoat and human-sacrifice ritual escapes the attention of most people, whether believers or unbelievers, as does the fact that the very premise of original sin is based on a *mythical motif.*

The first dictionary definition of "sin" is:

1. transgression of divine law: the sin of Adam.[1]

"Original sin" is defined as:

1. Theology.

> a. a depravity, or tendency to evil, held to be innate in humankind and transmitted from Adam to the race in consequence of his sin.

> b. inclination to evil, inherent in human nature.

2. Roman Catholic Theology. the privation of sanctifying grace in consequence of the sin of Adam.[2]

Original sin is described as that which resulted from the "Fall of Man," i.e., man's expulsion from the Garden of Eden, as depicted in the third chapter of  Genesis and as also termed the "sin of Adam," although usually attributed to Eve. Again, according to Christianity, this fall produced the state of sinfulness redeemable only through the sacrifice of Jesus. This transgression is also cited to justify a woman's pain in childbirth (Gen 3:16), as well as the harsh life destined for Adam and his descendants (Gen 3:17-19).

---

[1] *The Random House College Dictionary,* "sin."

[2] *The American College Dictionary,* 855.

## The Sin of Adam

The cause of the "Fall of Man," the "sin of Adam" is identified by the *Catholic Encyclopedia* (*"CE"*) also as "the origin of death," as at Romans 5:12. Adam's sin is reiterated at Romans 5:19: "For as by one man's disobedience many were made sinners..." The *CE* further relates that the apostle Paul interprets Adam's sin as passed along in the same way in which God made man to procreate, i.e., through sex: "Since Adam transmits death to his children by way of generation when he begets them mortal, it is by generation also that he transmits to them sin..."[1] Hence, we are all guilty by association, by our mere birth and existence.

Why would God create human beings in this manner? Why then does the all-powerful Lord of the cosmos need to engage in human sacrifice in order to fix his creature, poorly created by him in the first place? Can the Almighty not just snap his fingers and change humanity? If mankind's original sin is removed via a mystical and supernatural scapegoat ritual, i.e., the sacrifice of Jesus, why cannot some other mechanism equally as supernatural be utilized, such as that snap of the fingers? The Christian baptism too is supposed to remove magically the taint of original sin, but, as we can tell from the state of the

world, this mystical mumbo-jumbo has little to no effect. If baptism were effective, why conduct a brutal, bloody and barbaric human-sacrifice ritual, murdering God as his own son?

Additionally, it is the fruit of *the tree of knowledge of good and evil* that causes the initial fall, which means that God wants his creatures not to become knowledgeable but, rather, to remain ignorant. The knowledge of good and evil also leads Adam and Eve to "become ashamed of their nakedness." Man's—or, rather, *Eve's*—act in eating the

---

[1] *CE*, XI, 312.

fruit and thus becoming "as gods" (Gen 3:5) incurs an eternal penalty. So why does God put this tempting tree in the path of his innocent and ignorant creature in the first place? In this regard, the Gnostics believed that it was not *the* God of the cosmos but the lower, evil "demiurge" who was attempting to keep mankind ignorant, while the serpent was bringing wisdom.

In reality, there is no evidence for a Garden of Eden with an original couple who transgressed by eating a fruit from a magical tree, after being enticed by the devil in the form of a serpent. This story serves as a primitive and *mythical* attempt to explain why there is so much evil in the world, if there exists an all-good, all-perfect and all-powerful God in charge of everything. Hence, the devil is introduced, and the onus is largely put on Woman, leading to an unending and massive amount of sexism and misogyny over the millennia.

More than a thousand years after this story was first written in the Bible,[1] the Koran (2:30ff; 7:11-27) built upon this myth, and, although it does not teach "original sin" *per se*, Islam promulgates the same human-denigrating attitude as well. In a strange twist, however, Islam does not single out Eve to blame for the sin. (Q 7:24-25) Yet, an anti-human and sexist bias reveals itself in the massive amount of brutality, cruelty and violence of all levels in places where fundamentalism reigns. The disobedience introduced by the serpent/Satan includes disbelief in Islam, which means that non-Muslims are the most egregious sinners, explaining why they can be persecuted and

---

[1] See Finkelstein's *The Bible Unearthed* for the most scientific dating of biblical books: "...we know now that the early books of the Bible and their famous stories of early Israelite history were first codified (and in key respects composed) at an identifiable place and time: Jerusalem in the seventh century BCE." (Finkelstein, 5.)

killed readily and with impunity. Those who follow
Islam to the letter, with all of its harshness, will be the
most welcome in "paradise." Naturally, a thinking
person must wonder how such heartlessness is the
product of any "good" god, and what kind of "paradise"
or "heaven" would be populated by people who have
spent their lives in brutality, cruelty and violence?

### Sinners or Not?

The nature and meaning of "original sin" have been
debated for centuries among Christians and "heretics"
of a wide variety of sects. For instance, some claim
that the sin did not taint Adam's progeny for all
eternity, while many people believe that babies are
born in sin, but others do not. Some modern Christian
apologists go so far as to argue that none of us are
born in sin. However, without original sin there would
be no need for redemption through Jesus Christ. In
other words, if there is no sin, there is no need for a
savior. And, outside of Christianity, we are free not to
accept this interpretation of reality at all.

To those who know the true nature and potential of
the human being, this "born-in-sin" propaganda ranks
as calumny, slander and libel, pure and simple.
Human beings are *not* born in sin, and therefore there
is no need for a savior of any kind. It is by this
crippling belief in the first place that humanity
becomes sickened enough psychologically and
spiritually in order to need a savior to fix it. In other
words, the religion creates the disease and then
provides a "cure," which in reality is no cure at all but
serves as a placebo designed to keep mankind
enthralled to the same ideology for all eternity, if
possible.

This born-in-sin slur has led to an astonishing
amount of guilt, anger, hatred and violence on planet
Earth. People programmed with this belief automatically
assume that *all* human beings are sinners and thus
are immoral and deserving of denigration and
contempt. Hence, much libel, slander and defamation

of character can be traced to this born-in-sin dis-ease produced by fundamentalist Christianity.

The perception we may hold instead of this notion of people being "born in sin" wretches and pieces of garbage is that the human is a divine being who can attain to godly heights through innate morality, decency, kindness and love.

# Eternal Life for Everyone?

"The notion of the soul's eternal life is not new in Greek thought [with Plato]. It was expressed to some extent by Anaxagoras [c. 500-428 BCE], the Pythagoreans, and even such poets as Homer [9th cent. BCE?] and Pindar [c. 522-443 BCE]....."

Dr. Erich Segal, *The Dialogues of Plato* (xviii)

"Whoso eateth my flesh, and drinketh my blood, hath eternal life; and I will raise him up at the last day."

John 6:54

For thousands of years, people around the globe have believed in divine, immortal beings of one sort or another who supposedly appear on occasion to the faithful to bestow blessings and spiritual healings upon them. In various parts of the world in modern times, these alleged entities have taken on the form of the Judeo-Christian messiah and madonna, the many incarnations of God in the Hindu religion, the various Buddhas and Bodhisattvas as in the Tibetan religion, or any number of other deities worshipped and believed in globally. In ancient times, believers propitiated such gods as Zeus, Isis, Astarte, Apollo, Mithras, Horus and many others. There have been thousands of such godly creatures over the millennia;

indeed, Hinduism claims 333 million of them in its pantheon.[1]

## Divine Qualities are Not Restricted to the Divine

Within their traditions and mythologies, what all of these figures have in common are immortality, supernatural powers and the ability to appear third-dimensionally now and again. In fact, these qualities have come to define what the average human being considers to be God, or at least an aspect of God, whether as "his son" or some other rendition. With the attribution of such sacred qualities, the human being also bestows a great deal of respect and adulation upon these seemingly divine creatures. Because the average person considers him or herself separate from God, he or she does not believe that he or she possesses any such supernatural or divine powers. The common folk often believe themselves to be helpless, pitiful creatures who must rely on outside intervention to have a reasonably good life.

Yet, the standard religious doctrine also teaches that if the lowly human being is very good, behaves himself and "believes unto the Lord," he will earn eternal life. It is likewise widely believed that certain of the biblical "prophets," such as Elijah and Moses, were able to attain to this status of immortality, as their appearance from the otherworld next to the "son of Man" was purported in the New Testament. (Mk 9:4) Thus, it is obvious that even mortals can attain to immortality, according to this belief system.

Our religions have also taught that numerous people have been able to develop supernatural powers

---

[1] Giddens, 15. This number represents a well-known claim within Hinduism. It does not reflect an actual figure from someone counting the various gods but is said to represent the population of India at the time it was devised.

such as those attributed to Jesus. For example, in the New Testament book of Acts, the disciples are able to heal the sick and do other miracles (e.g., Acts 3:6ff). Deceased saints too are imagined to be working their healing magic eternally from the "other side," while televangelists pretend likewise to do supernatural healings. Supernatural apparitions of dead prophets, saints and "common people" as ghosts have also been contended over the millennia. According to such traditions, then, it is apparent that mere mortals have also been able to develop powers deemed divine.

## Join the Crowd—Everyone is God

All of this speculation leaves one to ask, if immortality, supernatural powers and the ability to appear mystically in the third dimension from the other side are signs of divinity, can we not then assume that every human being who "through faith" has attained to eternal life, developed spiritual gifts and has revealed him or herself in apparitions or voices after death is also to be considered God or the son/ daughter of God? Many religious people who have been taught to believe that Jesus alone is the true face of divinity also often claim that they have heard the voices of their deceased loved  ones or have seen ghosts of them or some other such vision. Obviously, these religious people would also hope that their departed had been "saved," i.e., accepted Jesus Christ as their Savior, and therefore would be guaranteed eternal life. What differentiates their departed loved ones from angels or even the son of God or God himself? What makes God or Jesus any different from these dead people, who have now attained to immortality, have developed supernatural powers and possess the ability to contact the living?

Aren't they on the same plane as God and Jesus? Are they not also *divine* in essence?

## Uncle Harry is Immortal!

To say that "God" or the Divine has one face, or a specific gender, race or ethnicity, or is completely separate from us or our "immortal" deceased, flies in the face of the very notions that believers hold up as "God's Word." If all of the true believers—i.e., those who uncritically accept what a handful of men wrote down 2,000 or more years ago—who have ever died have been granted eternal life, i.e., immortality, that would pretty well put them on a par with God or his son or his mother or his aunt or any other immortal creature. If someone were to say that their long-dead uncle Harry appeared to them the other day and conveyed some godly information, and therefore was undoubtedly God himself, who could prove them wrong? Let us, therefore, recognize that he, we and the entire cosmos are divine.

# Holy Days

"Of course, I am in favor of everybody keeping holidays to suit himself, provided he does not interfere with others, and I am perfectly willing that everyone should go to church on that day, provided he is willing that I should go elsewhere."

Colonel Robert G. Ingersoll, *The Works of Robert G. Ingersoll* (XI, 433)

What are holidays? Year after year, throngs of people of all religions and sects march off to their temples, churches, synagogues and mosques to celebrate "holidays," the origins of which many of these same individuals are often completely unaware. How many Christians know, for example, that "Christmas"—which they believe marks the birthday of a messiah sent by a father-god figure—is actually the day when the sun, from a geocentric perspective, begins its journey north again after passing through the winter solstice? Do all these Christians who take off Christmas to celebrate the little babe in the manger realize they are marking a *Pagan* holiday commemorating the movements of the sun?[1] Few people realize that Hanukkah, which may be understood as a very important time in the eyes of the Jewish deity, Yahweh, was actually created to "combat" the religious holiday of the Christians, who in turn borrowed theirs

---

[1] See, e.g., my book *Christ in Egypt*, 83ff.

from the Pagans.[1] And so on, through the list of holidays of many cultures and religions.

## Look to the Stars—"Religion" is Based on Astrotheology

Traditionally from ancient times, many religious holidays have been founded on the movements of the celestial bodies, and not on anyone's birth, death, racial history, winning of battles, exoduses out of bondage, etc. Indeed, these latter assumed religious holidays have represented little more than competitions between the assorted creeds and sects. As such, they are not days of great importance to a male god person sitting in his castle in the clouds, instead constituting egotistical and ethnocentric moves by competitors in the fields of politics and religion. And, again, there is no god person sitting "up there" watching and nodding his head in approval at the commemoration of these supposed holy days.

In other words, as purported commemorations of something sacred to God, these holidays are fraudulent. If they were truthfully recognizing the movements of the planetary bodies, as well as other aspects of nature worship, such as the "Pagans" do still today, they would not be fraudulent, because such were the original "holy days" beginning in antiquity.

---

[1] See Marcus, 110.

As they are currently presented, therefore, many holidays are bogus, in that they do not really represent days sacred to God. There are many people who can see the ethnocentricity and bigotry involved in these holidays; however, even they may go along with them, perhaps thinking that if there is an anthropomorphic deity somewhere "out there" they may be able to win  points in his Book of Life and Death. Let us develop or *re-develop* truly universal holidays not based on how many other cultures we have trounced, how many people we have slaughtered, the day "our Lord" was viciously murdered or our prophet suffered martyrdom, or some other such violent and life-denying thing. Let us abandon such ugly concepts and instead create beautiful celebrations of humankind, the rest of the natural world and the awesome vastness of the cosmos.

# The Origins of Good and Evil

"This difficulty of 'good' and 'evil,' the crux of all philosophy, has been approached by mystical thinkers in various ways...but the boldest of them...have attacked the problem directly, and carrying mystical thought to its logical conclusion, have unhesitatingly asserted that God is the origin of Good and Evil alike, that God and the devil, in short, are but two sides of the same Force."

Dr. Caroline F.E. Spurgeon, *Mysticism in English Literature* (96)

Around the world there are a variety of cultures with an assortment of religious beliefs and systems. Within these different cultures and religious ideologies appear varied perceptions of what is real in the universe. Some of them have a deity or deities; some have no god. The diversity is great. Many of the deities are anthropomorphic, others are animalistic; some are elemental, and others have no form. Many traditions possess the concept of good and evil; others do not. Those traditions that do not separate out good and evil, such as Taoism, consider all things in the universe, whether viewed as good or evil, to be within the cosmic plan or mind that some call "God." In other words, in some views, "God" is simply a term to describe the entire universe and all its aspects, whether good or evil.

The question arises, where have the concepts of good and evil come from, since they have developed so differently around the globe? Why is it that some cultures view some things as evil while others see them as good, and vice versa? How can followers of one religion believe that only those individuals who hold the identical tenets are good, while those who do not are evil? Since no one religion is followed by a majority of the earth's inhabitants, how can such followers view the rest of the world's population as doing the devil's work? Where did these ideas originate? Are they based in reality? Is there a good god and an evil devil who take turns influencing the universe and our world? Who determines which is which? How did this determination come about?

## Narrow Perceptions Represent Bigotry

For those people who study the subject in depth, and have insights of their own, the answer becomes clear as to what is going on. What becomes obvious is that each group has conditioned itself to believe it holds the only truth, way and path. Many religions and cults believe that those who do not view reality their way are doomed to hell by their chosen deity. Most religions hold that if their specific guidelines are not followed, true salvation will not occur. What becomes abundantly evident about these religious systems to those who seriously involve themselves from as unprejudiced a perspective as is possible—say, that of an alien visitor simply observing this planet—is that they are not based on true revelation from any specific deity who is the absolute authority and who gives "his word" to "his chosen people," but instead are often founded upon ethnocentric and cultural biases designed to bring political and material gain to those who can force them upon others.

This statement may seem shocking to those who have not looked into the situation to any extent. Those who are caught up in any given religious tradition will believe that their system is the only true one, the most advanced and correct in the universe. This belief represents the first sign of egotism and arrogance. This notion presupposes that no other group of people or individual has ever possessed an enlightened or wise thought. This perception assumes that only those who carry "the way, the truth and the life" (Jn 14:6) according to "sacred texts" have any intelligence or morality whatsoever. It also presumes that whoever received "the Word" in the first place is an egotistical "chosen person," megalomaniacal "son of God," a conceited "most perfect man" or some such.

## True Wisdom can be Found Anywhere, Not Just in Some Old Book

The fact is that around the world wisdom has been

able to penetrate the noggins of a multitude of people, to be revealed in a large array of creative ideas. Contrary to what fanatic religionists would have everyone believe, there is nothing at all wrong with this variety. This variety is the spice of life, and those who avail themselves of it are greatly enriched in consciousness and spirit. Those who narrow down their consciousness to reject the wisdom and perception of all other cultures in favor of their own egotistical and ethnocentric "religious" beliefs are often mean-spirited and poorly educated yet very conceited. They call themselves devout, but they are really out of it.

## "Religions" are Recycled Myths

As an example of how religious dogma is derived from political and material gain, let us look at the Western tradition of good and evil as held by the Judeo-Christian-Islamic/Abrahamic traditions. Many people think that these systems come out of a "unique" Hebraic interpretation of God/Devil, which was revealed directly from God. What few realize is that the Hebraic interpretation represents a lift from older cultures such as the Phoenician, Babylonian, Sumerian, Zoroastrian, Indian and Egyptian. A study of the evolution of religion reveals that numerous cultures have borrowed various spiritual traditions of other cultures and reworked them to revolve around themselves. This assertion is particularly true regarding cultures that have merged through invasion. Throughout the past 6,000 years of known history peoples have migrated and

moved all over the place, so much so that it is impossible here to name the migrations. During these various migrations, which were often caused by the need to find better, less exploited, more fertile territory, invaders absorbed the cultures they invaded. To accomplish this assimilation, they often had to make the presiding cultural gods either into sub-deities under their own god or gods, or into demons and devils. This development is precisely what has occurred throughout the world, whether or not one realizes that fact.

### Abraham is Brahma? Moses is Dionysus?

In the case of the Hebraic tradition, the Semitic group of people who later became known as Jews engulfed and incorporated into its pantheon of prophets, patriarchs and deities the gods of other cultures, such as Brahma, the Indian creator god, who evidently became the patriarch Abraham; or Mises, the Greco-Phoenician superhuman hero-lawgiver, who apparently was morphed into the

prophet Moses. Concerning Abraham, in *Essential Hinduism*, Steven J. Rosen relates:

> The similarities between the names Abraham and Brahma have not gone unnoticed. Abraham is said to be the father of the Jews, and Brahma, as the first created being, is often seen as the father of mankind.... Some say that the word *Abraham* is derived from the Sanskrit word *brahma*...[1]

Rosen goes on to clarify that the two words are probably unrelated etymologically. However, the root of *brahma*, *brah*, does mean "to grow or multiply in number,"[2] while Abraham was said to be the "father of multitudes" (Gen 17:5). Moreover, there are a number of other intriguing correspondences between the two characters, including that the wife of Abraham was Sarah, while Brahma's consort was Sarasvati.[3] The presence of the Indian language of Vedic in the Mitanni kingdom of Asia Minor around 3,500 years ago,[4] and the assertion by the Jewish historian Josephus (*Against Apion*, I) that the Greek philosopher Aristotle claimed the Jews were descendants of "Indian philosophers,"[5] lend further credence to this contention.

Famed Israelite prophet Moses too appears to be not a historical figure but a mythical character replicated in a number of cultures. For example, regarding the Greek god Dionysus/Bacchus, in *The Diegesis*, Rev. Dr. Robert Taylor relates:

> In the ancient Orphic verses sung in the orgies of Bacchus, as celebrated throughout Egypt, Phoenicia,

---

[1] Rosen, 12.
[2] Rosen, 12.
[3] Kinsley, 55.
[4] Anthony, 49.
[5] Josephus/Whiston, 487.

Syria, Arabia, Asia Minor, Greece, and ultimately in Italy, it was related how *that* God, who had been born in Arabia, was picked up in a box that floated on the water, and took his name *Mises*, in signification of his having been "saved from the water," and *Bimater*, from his having had two mothers; that is, one by nature, and another who had adopted him. He had a rod with which he performed miracles, and which he could change into a serpent at pleasure. He passed the Red Sea dry-shod, at the head of his army. He divided the waters of the rivers Orontes and Hydraspus, by the touch of his rod, and passed through them dry-shod. By the same mighty wand, he drew water from the rock; and wherever he marched, the land flowed with wine, milk, and honey.[1]

Thus, we discover traditions attached to Dionysus/Bacchus, also called Iacchus and *Mises*, that in essence represent the story of Moses, full of fantasy and fabulous exploits which are better taken as myth than history.

In the writings of the earlier French scholar Voltaire we find the same basic information:

> The ancient poets have placed the birth of Bacchus in Egypt; he is exposed on the Nile and it is from that event that he is named Mises by the first Orpheus, which, in Egyptian, signifies "saved from the waters"... He is brought up near a mountain of Arabia called Nisa, which is believed to be Mount Sinai. It is pretended that a goddess ordered him to go and destroy a barbarous nation and that he passed through the Red Sea on foot, with a multitude of men, women, and children. Another time the river Orontes suspended its waters right and left to let him pass, and the Hydaspes did the same. He commanded the sun to stand still; two luminous rays proceeded from his head. He made a

---

[1] Taylor, R., 190-191. In Knight, we find reference to "the *Mises* or Bacchus *Diphues* [two-natured]..." (Knight, 90.)

fountain of wine spout up by striking the ground with his thyrsis, and engraved his laws on two tables of marble. He wanted only to have afflicted Egypt with ten plagues, to be the perfect copy of Moses.[1]

Voltaire likewise names others preceding him who had made this comparison between Moses and Dionysus/Bacchus, such as the Dutch theologian Gerhard Johann Voss/Vossius (1577–1649), whose massive study of mythology has never been translated from the Latin,[2] and Pierre Daniel Huet (1630-1721), the Bishop of Avranches. Another commentator was French novelist Charles-Antoine-Guillaume Pigault-Lebrun or "Le Brun" (1753-1835), who in his *Doubts of Infidels* remarked:

> The history of Moses is copied from the history of Bacchus, who was called Mises by the Egyptians, instead of Moses. Bacchus was born in Egypt; so was Moses... Bacchus passed through the Red Sea on dry ground; so did Moses. Bacchus was a lawgiver; so was Moses. Bacchus was picked up in a box that floated on the water; so was Moses.... Bacchus by striking a rock made wine gush forth... Bacchus was worshipped...in Egypt, Phenicia, Syria, Arabia, Asia and Greece, before Abraham's day.[3]

The name "Moses" is said to mean "drawn out" in Hebrew but "born of" in Egyptian.[4] Indeed, the Egyptian term for "birth" is basically *ms* or *mes*,[5] while in Coptic it is *mise*,[6] such that it is highly

[1] Voltaire, 186; Morley, 191.

[2] Vossius, *De theologia gentili et physiologia Christiana, De origine et progressu idololatriae.*

[3] Draper, 514; Pigault-Lebrun, 19-20. The original of this work was in French and was called *Le Citateur.* An English translation was included in a volume with the peculiar title of *An Eye-Opener, "Citateur, par Pigault." Le Brun, Doubts of Infidels,* by someone named "Zepa."

[4] Nohrnberg, 135.

[5] Collier, 155;

[6] Allen, 9.

believable Dionysus would share such a title, especially when one considers that he was deemed an Egyptian god in ancient times[1] and that Egyptian words are often transliterated with different vowels. The equation of Moses with Bacchus becomes even more likely when one considers that in an ancient Orphic hymn in Greek invoking Dionysus (42)—undoubtedly that to  which Voltaire referred—the god is said to be the offspring of the "Good Counselor of a hundred names, and the pure and holy Mise..."[2] Dr. David M. Halperin, et al., note that Mise, who is androgynous or "two-natured," is also associated with the goddess Kore or Persephone, as is the variant name *Mises*.[3] In another translation of this Orphic hymn, Dionysus/Iacchus is addressed as "Mises, ineffable, pure..."[4] *Mises* is also mentioned by the ancient Greek poet Herodas in the third century BCE.[5]

In *Jones' Dictionary of Old Testament Proper Names*, theologian Rev. Alfred Jones cites Bishop Dr. Simon/Symon Patrick (1626-1707) as commenting:

> ...in Orpheus's hymns, Bacchus is called Mises, which seems to be the same with Moses; out of whose story all that the Greeks and others say of Bacchus seems to have been framed.[6]

---

[1] Herodotus (2.47); Herodotus/Waterfield, 114.
[2] Halperin, 100.
[3] Halperin, 100, 103.
[4] Orpheus/Taylor, T., 141. Taylor lists the pertinent hymn as "XLI" or 41, whereas more modern sources cite it as 42.
[5] Herodas, 10.
[6] Jones, 189. In discussing 1 Samuel 6:19, which relates to the tale of the men of Bethshemesh, who were killed after looking into the Ark of the Covenant, Bishop Patrick asserts: "Out of this story, as *Bocharius* [Samuel Bochart (1599-1667)] ingeniously conjectures, the *Greeks* forged the Fable of *Bacchus*, who was very angry with the *Athenians*, because they did not receive his Mysteries with Pomp, when they were brought out of *Boeotia* into *Attica*, and smote them with a sore Disease in their Secret Parts." (Patrick, 70.)

Naturally, this Christian authority and others attempted to make the Greeks the borrowers of the Hebrew myth, rather than the other way around. Nevertheless, the comparisons appear to be sound—and in need of further scientific study to discern which is the borrower and which the originator.

### God and the Devil are One

The God/Devil characters of the Old Testament are also derived in this way from older traditions, especially the Egyptian and Zoroastrian. In fact, the God/Devil construct largely constitutes a derivation of the dual God of Persia, Ahura-Mazda and his "twin" Ahriman,[1] or the Egyptian Horus/Set.[2] Set and Horus, for example, at one point represented the dark and light aspects of the one God, among many other attributes. Set or Seth was the primary god in a number of very ancient cultures along the Nile River. Set eventually came to be the god of

the south, where his peoples resided. At that time, Horus was only a vague entity somewhere to the north. As the peoples migrated towards the north, Set, as symbolized by the South Pole star, began to become less and less visible, and it came to be believed that Set was descending into the underworld to become God there.[3]

Sooner or later, the story goes, as the people continued to migrate north and became more focused on the Lord of the North Pole star, Horus, they began to view Set as less important and Horus of greater significance. No doubt this led to conflicts. Set continued to be worshipped along the Nile, but it became clear that factions arose who desired to make

---

[1] See, e.g., Freedman: "Some scholars see Zoroastrianism as the source of dualistic thinking in Judaism." (Freedman, 1424.)

[2] See my book *Christ in Egypt: The Horus-Jesus Connection.*

[3] Massey, I, 268-269.

Horus supreme. This ploy would be, once again, for political and material reasons. The movements of the astral bodies that corresponded with and symbolized these entities, such as the pole stars, as well as other celestial bodies, were crucial to life along the Nile. These heavenly bodies were closely charted and calendared. Such movements provided a semblance of order in what would ordinarily seem like a chaotic and unkind world full of yearly flooding, terrible sandstorms and unbearable heat. By measuring the movements of such celestial bodies, those who later became regarded as priests could determine when would be the most auspicious time for planting and harvesting. This situation was intrinsic to life along the Nile, and without it there was no survival.

If, as happens frequently in history, some sort of natural disaster were to strike a particular culture, group or people, the priests would look towards the displeasure of the god behind any one of the various celestial bodies or elemental forces such as wind, which was represented by the Egyptian "Shu," for example. The priests would then determine that such a deity needed to be  propitiated so that order would return to the world. The priests would sometimes battle as to which god would be appeased, and during difficult transitions— for example, in the era when Horus came to usurp Set in importance—these conflicts could become ugly and violent. Indeed, priests of various religions have resorted to all sorts of name-calling, propaganda and violence to make sure their particular interpretation was set in stone. In the case of Horus and Set, Set— who was once considered an equal of his twin brother Horus—became viewed as something bad or evil. Set, as "Prince of Darkness," so to speak, and "Serpent of the Underworld,"[1] came to be seen as an enemy of the people. This characterization likely in part developed because of the fear of the dark and the insecurities felt throughout the night. But, as can be evidenced by the story of the Greek god Hades, the "Lord of the Underworld" was not always viewed by all peoples as evil. Hades was, in fact, simply another god doing his job. It was thus a certain bias that eventually led to the establishment of the Prince of Darkness and Lord of the Underworld as an evil and sinister character.

### "Evil" is Subjective

Speaking of sinister, how many people realize that

the word "sinister" actually means "left" in Latin? Indeed, in Latin "left," "on the left," "on the left hand" or "at the left side" is *sinister* or *sinistra*, also meaning "wrong" or "perverse."[2] "Left" is also *sinistra* in Italian. Here is a classic example of how cultural bias has attached a judgment to something so simple and benign as a direction, view or aspect. And how did this judgment come about? Left-handers, it seems, were considered dangerous to the status quo, possibly because their use of the left appendage kept the creative, right side of the brain open, leading to new and dangerous ideas—to creativity and union with the creator itself! Because these new ideas upset the status quo and could lead to its reduction in wealth and position, left-handers, or "leftists," were considered bad and evil. Hence, they became "sinister."

It is possible that the word "evil" itself is also derived from something equally innocuous but through cultural bias has become judged as something bad. Some claim "evil" has its roots in "Eve," or the

---

[1] Jackson, S., 368.
[2] Cassell's, 557; Lewis, 786.

primary female.[1] In this possible circumstance of etymological development, the aggressive male ego may have worked to make things of Eve bad or "evil."

In any event, although it was not previously this way, and in some places he is still revered—leading critics to make claims of "devil worship"—Set came to be viewed as something bad and evil. He eventually was seen as the cause of all problems to the peoples along the lower or northerly Nile. That he was not always viewed by all peoples as evil is exhibited by the fact that several Egyptian pharaohs over the centuries called themselves "Seti." The pharaoh was considered the living embodiment of deity, to rule in the earthly place of the entity, whether it was Ra, Horus, Osiris or Set. The Nile kingdoms have a long and colorful history of such traditions.

### Horus and Set—Sound Familiar?

Where is all this rumination leading us and what does the Egyptian history have to do with the present interpretation of good and evil as defined by our current religious traditions? You may have guessed by now that Set, Set-Anubis, Set-An or Sata, was called "Satan" in another culture.[2] Likewise, Set's previously equal brother and twin aspect of the One God, Horus— also styled the "Savior" and the "Anointed,"

representing the "Light of the World" and the "Sun of God" that rescues the world from darkness (Set)—has come to be viewed as "All Good" in the Judaized/ Hellenized/Romanized version now named "Jesus Christ." As we have seen, the "good" Horus, was not always considered an adversary of his "evil" brother Set, and today's

---

[1] The word "evil" is also "evel" in Old/Middle English, Old Frisian and Kentish, for example.
[2] See my book *Christ in Egypt*.

story that the "Prince of Darkness" and "Serpent of the Underworld" is an evil demon working against a good "Prince of Light" and "Lord of Heaven" was not always so. At one point, these two aspects of the One were equivalent in divinity. They became judged and deemed to be either good or evil because of political, environmental and egotistical motives. As it turns out, the scenario of good and evil, light and dark, God and Devil has largely developed through cultural and political insights and biases, not through the revelation from a purely good deity.

The lesson of all of this discussion: Don't be too sure you know what good and evil are—and don't judge a person by the contents of The Book.

# The Devil is Divine

"To state the thing in brief, priests and politicians 'colleagued together,' and invented the Devil and his domicile as scare-crows to frighten the ignorant superstitious masses into quiet, submissive allegiance to the ecclesiastical tribunals, namely, 'the powers that be.'"

Kersey Graves, *The Biography of Satan: Exposing the Origins of the Devil* (108)

Do you know where the word "devil" comes from? Do you know how the Devil was created? Yes, created, because that is precisely what has happened. As opposed to something real and set in stone that mankind has merely perceived, the Devil is a creation of man's mind. Take, for example, the current impression of a man with horns and a pitchfork. This image is a compilation of characters from other mythologies, incorporating elements of the Greek god of nature Pan, for instance. As stated by Devil expert Dr. Jeffrey Burton Russell, a professor of History at the University of Southern California: "The iconographic influence of Pan upon the Devil is enormous."[1] What these statements mean is that the Devil is a not a real person of demonic nature running around the universe terrorizing people with his godlike but evil powers. Although there is evil in the cosmos—even "absolute evil"—the current construct that humans perceive as the "Evil One" represents an

---

[1] Russell, J., 126.

anthropomorphic version based in mythology. True evil is not personal, not a single being. It is a *quality* that can be possessed by anyone.

### The Origin of Evil

If you ask someone the question, "If God is so good, why is there so much evil in the world?," he or she may answer, "Because of the Devil." If you ask that believer, "Who created the Devil?," he may then

say that the Devil has always existed, not really wanting to ascribe such a malevolent creation to the all-good God. Of course, that eternal existence puts the Devil on a par with God, who was the original being from which all creation comes. Well then, the faithful may say, the Devil/ Satan/Lucifer was one of God's creatures that "got away from him"

or rebelled—the evil angel, as it were. But that contention nonetheless makes the Devil one of God's creatures, hardly a handiwork to be proud of. It also implies that God is not very powerful, in that he can lose control of his creatures so easily.

### How Religions are Made

In reality, the formed anthropomorphized entities currently portrayed as both God and the Devil are creations of the human being, not vice versa. That this assertion is true can be shown quite simply by using as illustration the evolution of religion. Religion, to those who have eyes to see and ears to hear, turns out not to be a divine revelation from any god person who created everything and knows all. In actuality, "religion" is a construct that often takes centuries and millennia to complete, beginning with various perceptions of the natural and "supernatural" worlds around us.

The first perception we have of the "supernatural hand of God" is elemental: the wind, the heat, the cold, the light, the dark, the rain, etc. Because the elements seem to have a mind of their own, human beings love to anthropomorphize them and give them human qualities. Thus, purely atmospheric phenomena come to be viewed as expressions of a humanlike entity that possesses sentience, in a development called either "nature worship" or "astrotheology," this latter term mainly applicable to the study and reverence of

the sun, moon, planets, earth, stars and constellations.

In humanity's nature-worshipping endeavors, we ascribe personality characteristics to the various entities we build up around the elements: For example, Zeus, the Greek sky-god father-figure, takes on a thunder-and-lighting personality.

This business is how religion evolves. Although religious fanatics may violently oppose this notion, much religion is basically mythology built upon limited human perceptions of what exists in the universe, and not upon concrete and absolute truths handed down by an omniscient god. Absolute truth has no form; hence, whenever "God" is portrayed as having form, whether human or animal, male or female, black, white or polka-dotted, such a depiction is not *the* Truth.

In looking at religion, what we find around the globe is a core mythos based on atmospheric elements and planetary bodies or other natural forces with a variety of forms they take on. In places where the skin of the inhabitants is red, the god may have red skin, and where the skin is white, the god may have white skin, and so on. The shape, form, gender and message of the god or *goddess* are often arbitrary, dependent on culture, environment and era, and not based on actual fact.

Frequently, different groups of people—and there have been very many cultures and groups on this planet—bring their distinct interpretations of deity to each other, whether through friendly merger or violent conquest, the latter of which seems to be the norm. During this merger process, the predominant people will force their particular, ethnocentric, egocentric and gender-centric interpretation of deity upon the conquered peoples. At the same time, they will also either make the conquered deities into lesser gods, godmen, heroes, prophets, patriarchs or saints in their own pantheon, or they will turn the conquered deity or deities into demons and devils.

## The Origin of the Words "Devil" and "Demon"

It has been said that the very words "devil" and "demon" have been vilified in just such a way as happens with the gods of other cultures being demoted or demonized. Before cultural judgment turned these  words into something wholly other than their original meaning, it is claimed, they represented entities considered sacred and holy. According to some, the word "devil" comes from the Sanskrit/Vedic word "deva," which shares the same root as "divine" and which refers to the good angels of the Hindu pantheon. This theory relates that it was only after the legendary prophet Zoroaster and the Persians conquered Hindu territory that they felt compelled to make the Hindu gods into devils! Thus, the Hindu devas became the Persians devils. As Rev. George William Cox (1827-1902) says:

> The Devas of the [Hindu] Veda are the bright gods
> who fight on the side of Indra; in the [Zoroastrian]
> Avesta the word has come to mean an evil spirit, and

the Zoroastrian was bound to declare that he ceased to be a worshipper of the daevas...

...the word devil passed into an immense number of forms, the Gothic tieval, diuval, diufal, the Icelandic djofull, Swedish djevful, all of them, together with the Italian, French, and Spanish forms carrying back the [Greek] word διαβολος [diabolos] to the same root which furnished the Latin Divus, Djovis, and the Sanskrit deva.[1]

We further read:

Thus the devils of Zoroaster were the gods of the older [Hindu] religion. This is indicated in the very word "devil." *Deva*, from which the word "devil" is derived, once meant the good gods. The same use remains today; for "divine" is only the old word *deva* in its modern dress. So "devil" and "divine" are two words coming from the same root. The same is true of Latin *deus* and our English "deity." In like manner the old Pagan gods became the devils of early and mediaeval Christianity; except when some infallible pope put one of them into the calendar by mistake, and made him a saint.[2]

Elsewhere from a modern Indian scholar we read:

The English word devil comes from the same root as deva; deva means god. Devil and god come from the same root: dev. Dev means light; from the same dev comes the devil; and from the same dev comes deva, devata, the divine. The words divine and devil come from the same Sanskrit root dev.[3]

The conversion of the Vedic deities to the Zoroastrian or Avestan devils is also related by Dr. George Rawlinson (1812-1902), a professor of Ancient History at Oxford and canon of Canterbury:

With respect to the evil spirits or intelligences, which, in the Zoroastrian system stood over against the good ones, the teaching of the early reformers

---

[1] Cox, 355, 363.
[2] Savage, 96.
[3] Osho, 101.

seems to have been less clear. The old divinities, except where adopted into the new creed, were in a general way called *Devas*, "fiends" or "devils," in contrast with the *Ahuras*, or "gods."[1]

Rawlinson notes, however, that there "is no etymological connection...between *deva* and 'devil.'" He continues:

> When...the Western Arians broke off from their brethren, and rejected the worship of their gods, whom they regarded as evil spirits, the word *deva*, which they specially applied to them, came to have an evil meaning, equivalent to our "fiend" or "devil." "Devil" is of course a mere corruption of διαβολος, Lat. *diabolus*...

Like Rawlinson, in *The Devil* Dr. Russell asserts that the words "devil" and "divine" are "totally unrelated etymologically."[2] According to current Western scholarship, then, the English term "devil" or "devel" is derived from the Greek *diabolos* and Latin *diabolus*, meaning "to slander" and "to hurl," whence the word "diabolical." The Indo-European roots of the two terms divine and devil are therefore different, the IE basis of "divine" being *deiw*, meaning "light," while "devil" originates in the IE *gwel*. It is curious, however, that if the word "devil" comes from *diabolos* and not *deva*, there would be two adjectives, i.e., "diabolical" *and* "devilish."

Adding to this assessment, Dr. Edwin Bryant, an associate professor of Religion at Rutgers University, states:

> In Sanskrit *deva* means "god" and *asura* means "demon." But in the Rigveda *asura* is also used as an epithet of some gods. In Iranian *deva* (Av *daeva*, OP *daiva*) means "devil/demon" and *asura* (Av and OP *ahura*) is used for "god." The word *deva* originally signifies god in Indo-European, cp Lat *deus* "god," Lith *devas* "god," etc. The Iranian use of *deva* "devil"

---

[1] Rawlinson, 104.
[2] Russell, J., 34.

is definitely an innovation. It is quite natural that when the Indo-Aryan and Iranians differed from each other dialectically and could not remain amicable, the Iranians left for Iran and settled there. There they might have developed an extremely antagonistic attitude toward the Indo-Aryans (who remained in India) and consequently in Iranian the use of the words *deva* and *asura* was reversed, which resulted in special sets of words called *ahura* and *daeva* in Avestan.[1]

This debate centers on whether the word "devil" comes from "deva," meaning "God," or from "diabolus/diabolos," with opinions on both sides. Indo-European is, of course, a speculative language, although modern

 scholarship regarding it is generally sound and scientific. As stated, "devil" in Sanskrit is listed as *asura*, which in the older Vedic means "divine" and "good spirit,"[2] the same as

*ahura* in the Persian language of Avestan. Once more, then, we find ourselves at the same place of one man's devil being another's angel. Hence, regardless of whether or not the deva/devil pun has etymological validity, it remains a "happy coincidence" that this play on words does in fact reflect a genuine cultural phenomenon: Again, one culture's gods are another's devils.

Likewise, the word "demon" unquestionably comes from the Greek word "daimon" or "daemon," which originally referred to beings of divine, godly nature—gods, not evil spirits.[3] The Greek word for

---

[1] Bryant, *IAC*, 211. "Av" is Avestan, the Persian language of the Zoroastrian texts, while "OP" stands for Old Persian.
[2] Monier-Williams, 121.
[3] Russell, J., 142.

"bad spirits" is transliterated *cacodaemon* or *kakodaimon*.[1] "Daemon" was thus corrupted and changed into having an evil connotation through the same religion-making process. It had nothing to do with an accurate discernment of any genuine evil spirit. It was simply Christian propaganda used to cause the followers of the Greek and Roman religions to reject their old gods in favor of the newly created Christian figure. As has been shown, this priestcraft is a very old trick. It was done rather well this time, with the subsequent burning of thousands of books, many of which would have revealed the ruse.

### In God's Name—Not the Devil's

In light of the fact that so-called holy scriptures record one barbarous, murderous act after another attributed to "God," it is not surprising that the "Devil" was once considered divine! Perhaps the Devil brings peace, and not a sword, to humanity. Considering how many people have been killed in the name of God and not the Devil, maybe the world is worshipping the wrong entity. Perhaps the Indians and the Greeks were right in the first place. Think about it: No army has ever marched off to war in the name of the Devil.[2]

---

[1] Rose, 59.

[2] These remarks represent a tongue-in-cheek critique of humanity's long and massive history of cruelty and barbarism in the name of God, not an actual call to devil worship, an utterly nonsensical notion some Satan-obsessed religionists may speciously claim.

# Prophecy or Blueprint?

"'But all this has taken place, that the scriptures of the prophets might be fulfilled.' Then all the disciples forsook him and fled."

Matthew 26:56

"Hide the prophecy, tell the narrative, and invent the history."

Dr. John D. Crossan, *The Historical Jesus* (372)

For thousands of years humanity has been fascinated by the study of prophecy or predictions of the future. Politically and in religious circles, it has been believed that the one who can divine the future holds tremendous power, and even the "little people" have desired to know what the future would hold for them, whether they would be rich or poor, whom they would marry, how many children they would have, if they would live long and how they would die.

Ascertaining the future has been a pursuit of millions around the globe, from purported diviners and seers such as Nostradamus and Edgar Cayce to the more mundane astrologers who compose general forecasts for the newspapers. Thus, considering such widespread interest in the future, whenever any prognostication has appeared to be accurate, to whatever

NOSTRADAMUS

degree, mankind has been held spellbound by the diviner or prediction itself.

## The Bible

Such has been the case with the so-called Word of God, the Judeo-Christian bible. For centuries to millennia since this tome was compiled, people have been attempting to associate the Bible's "predictions" or "prophecies" with events occurring in their own lifetimes. Particular individuals who are especially powerful and may find their way into history—such as noted politicians or religious figures—apparently have studied the Bible and its purported prophecies.

Curious humans continue to pore over the Bible in order to ascertain the future, and when something happens that can in some way be construed to validate supposed predictions from the "Good Book," its adherents cheer the incident as a sign of the legitimacy of "God's Word" and the omniscience of its alleged author. In other words, it is the duty of the biblical prophecy scholar to take global occurrences and make them fit as proof of the "fulfillment of prophecy," thus proving to himself and others that their religion and holy scriptures are accurate, correct and infallible. If believers are able to convince themselves that something has been predicted by their sacred book, they can confirm that they hold the correct belief system, as opposed to their neighbors, who may not be of the same faith. Whenever such an event has been interpreted to conform to the "prophecies" found in sacred scriptures, it proves to the believers that their way is the only right one. Thus, it behooves believers to interpret the world's affairs to agree with any perceived prognostication they may be able to find within their chosen book of faith.

Many cultures around the world have prophecies and predictions for the future. Each generation may take such prognostications and determine that they have occurred or will occur within its lifetime.

Armageddon and the Second Coming of Christ have been "just around the corner" practically since the New Testament was written. The supposed prophecies in the mysterious and strange biblical book of Revelation, for example, have been referred to and misinterpreted

constantly throughout the centuries. Unbeknownst to the masses, religious leaders and secular rulers alike have consulted Revelation, as well as the Old Testament Book of Daniel and other parts of the Bible, to discover whether they were mentioned in it. These leaders also wanted to figure out where their reign would go according to "God's Word." Over the course of history, powerful potentates in Christendom have engaged biblical scholars to study the Book and interpret its findings to apply to said rulers. It was the duty of just such an expert to find where in the Bible a leader or his nation may be discussed, and this interpretation obviously could lead to a great deal of skewing of the information found in the Good Book.

The questions relevant to us today include: Are

biblical prophecies, such as the "Mark of the Beast" at Revelation 13:16-17, coming true today? Have they ever come true? Does this apparent "fulfillment of prophecy" prove that

the Bible is the omniscient Word of God? The answer is, of course, no. The negative response is not to say that such a thing as the "Mark of the Beast" is not a reality occurring today, as the embedded computer chip claimed by biblical prophecy buffs to represent the mark certainly is real. However, such an occurrence does *not* rank as a fulfillment of prophecy that proves the Bible to be the accurate and infallible Word of God. This "no" also does not mean that certain happenings in the past have not somewhat coincided with statements found within the pages of the Bible. Most of the pronouncements pointed to in the Bible as "prophecies" have been so obscure and difficult to understand—because *they are frequently not prophecy at all*—that they can be and have been twisted to apply to anything zealots wish, just so the proselytizers can prove that their scriptures are the sole sacred texts in the world, the only books actually written by God himself. Naturally, of course, followers of the Koran believe the same thing about their sacred scriptures, which, like the Bible, contain some very *ungodly* sentiments, such as calling for the deaths of non-believers and the subjugation of women.[1]

## A Blueprint for Destruction

The reason why incidents that sometimes resemble biblical "predictions" represent neither fulfillment of prophecy nor proof that the sacred scriptures are the Word of God is because, in the first place, such events habitually have been misconstrued and fudged to fit the scripture and, in the second place, rulers and priests who lived when a particular "prophecy-fulfilling" instance supposedly has happened were often enough avid students of biblical predictions and may actually *cause* events to come to pass so that they could be considered to have been mentioned in the Book. What this assertion means is that those who have held the power to create on this planet have used the Bible as a *blueprint* that they would cause to pass to whatever extent. By adhering to biblical edict, not only could these rulers gain entrance into history, but they could also then smugly and self-righteously sit back and pronounce that their religion and their God were correct. This "validation" of their faith would then give them leeway to destroy other cultures around the

---

[1] See, e.g., Q 2:89-2:90, 4:34, 9:73, etc.

globe in the "Name of God." According to these fanatics, since certain biblical predictions had come to pass, this purported fulfillment of prophecy proved their inherent right to rule as upholders of the faith and gods upon Earth.

## Israel—God Gets His Favorite Vacation Spot Back

Today's bibliolaters point to the modern formation of Israel as a "fulfillment of prophecy" that signifies the beginning of the "End Times" and the Second Coming of Christ. They claim that the re-establishment of Israel was preordained by "God's infallible Word" and ultimately caused by God Almighty himself.

To assert that this occurrence constitutes a fulfillment of prophecy as opposed to a contrived following of a blueprint assumes that those who contributed to the modern establishment of Israel had never read the Bible or heard about its purported prophecies. Obviously, considering the importance given this book—which we are told represents the world's best-selling tome—it is a preposterous notion to presume that these powerful world leaders had never heard of the passages relating to the re-creation of Israel. Those who had a hand in forming Israel—many of whom were Bible-reading Jews and Christians—were undoubtedly well aware of the passages in the Bible regarding that nation. As the leaders in the past have adhered to the blueprint of the Bible in order to "prove" its assumed truthfulness, these modern determiners of destiny deliberately created Israel for a number of reasons, including to "fulfill prophecy" according to their chosen scriptures. There was nothing supernatural or divinely ordained about it. And, by the way, how come there's no mention in the "inerrant word of God" about *how* Israel would be formed, at the point of Hitler's pitchfork? Such a monumental oversight for a book that supposedly contains everything that ever has been and ever will be!

## Was Chernobyl a Can of Worms?

The implosion of the nuclear power plant in 1986 at Chernobyl, Russia, was likewise claimed to be a "fulfillment of prophecy" because the word "Chernobyl" allegedly means "Wormwood," as in the biblical passage of Revelation 8:11: "And the name of the star is called Wormwood: and the third part of the waters became wormwood; and many men died of the waters, because they were made bitter."

Rather than this tragic accident serving as a sign of supernatural intervention, it may be that those who placed the catastrophic nuclear plant at Chernobyl were also aware of this excerpt from Revelation. Since many ruling parties upon this planet have practiced the occult, which includes biblical prophecy, it may have been with tremendous irony that they contrived to position a poorly constructed nuclear reactor at such a site. However, the wormwood *plant* purportedly surrounds the Chernobyl reactor, and was supposedly the reason the area was so named, although there is a debate as to this interpretation of the city's name, which literally translates to "black white." If the scenario of "Chernobyl" meaning "wormwood" is true, this "coincidence" would actually be humorous, except that the event has been a toxic nightmare. So, if Chernobyl *was* an act of the all-powerful God following a biblical "prophecy"—and we may as well blame it on him as his followers are claiming he ordained it—it would reflect more sadism than humor.

## The Mark of the Beast & 666—an Evil Conspiracy?

In the past couple of decades, we have heard much about the "Mark of the Beast" as it is being applied in computer technology and bar codes that are, according to "insiders," destined to be placed in or upon the hands or foreheads of every man, woman and child on the planet. Biblical prophecy enthusiasts claim that the bar codes have within them the number "666" (a number, by the way, which was held sacred by Goddess-worshipping cultures before it was demonized by the patriarchy[1]) and that they are designed to be placed somewhere in the human body in order to track everyone on Earth and provide a new monetary system. The fact that this activity is already being done with animals, who are being implanted with electronic chips containing an access number that can be raised on a computer to reveal their owner's name and address, and also reportedly is being done with criminals, has been raised by prophecy fans to conclude that their faith and scriptures are not only correct but also wondrously omniscient, proof of their divine origin.

What these "experts" fail to acknowledge is that the originators of these various systems and technologies may also be versed well enough in biblical "prophecy" and be consciously bringing it to fulfillment. It is quite possible that when this chip technology began to take shape these designers decided the relevant passages in Revelation were a terrific idea for its application. This development would then constitute not fulfillment of prophecy but, rather, the completion of a *blueprint* that has been widely available to all in power for thousands of years. The keepers of this blueprint—the texts that make up the Bible—have frequently been members of secret societies and brotherhoods that

---

[1] Walker, 401.

make it their business to follow the Bible and its "predictions." There is nothing mysterious or supernatural about it. And their manmade achievements in bringing these plans to fruition do not prove the blueprint to be "fulfillment of prophecy."

### Since When is Building a Building "Fulfillment of Prophecy?"

If a building is constructed according to a blueprint, is it a great fulfillment of prophecy? No, it is merely a mechanical action taken by those who have the power to build it. To construct a building according to a blueprint implies no supernatural or godly intervention at all. It simply signifies that some person or persons have complied with a blueprint. In the case of biblical "prophecy," what is the vast temptation for the political and clerical power-mongers to deceive themselves and others by subsequently proclaiming their various deliberate constructions a "fulfillment of prophecy?" They can then claim for themselves a place in history as has been "predicted" by what is held by millions around the world to be "God's Word" but which is in reality just another book.

The Bible is not the "Word of God," nor is it a marvelous prognosticator that we should all heed. The Book of Revelation, which is so often pointed to as a prediction of the future, is not even originally a Judeo-Christian text but is part of a *genre* and has its origins in Egypt, Persia and India, as long as 4,000 years ago.[1] In *Ancient Egypt: The Light of the*

---

[1] Egyptologist Dr. Samuel Sharpe says: "In the Book of Revelation...written in the year A.D. 69, we find many traces of the Gnostic or at least Egyptian opinions." (Sharpe, 96.) This 4,000-year figure is based on the fact that the Egyptian Pyramid Texts began to appear at approximately that time.

*World*, lay Egyptologist Gerald Massey remarks:

> ...in the Book of Revelation the drama of the mysteries has been mistaken for human history, and a mythical catastrophe for the actual ending of the world. The book as it stands has no intrinsic value and very little meaning until the fragments of ancient lore have been collated, correlated, and compared with the original mythos and eschatology of Egypt.[1]

During this long span since it was written down or reworked in the second century of the common era, Revelation's "prophecies" have been perceived to have come true many times, even though the book itself was never meant to be a prophecy but represents an astronomical and astrological record.[2]

## Peace on Earth Requires Clarity of Perception, Not Belief

It is time for the world to wake up to the manipulations of both the history-hungry political leaders and the religious zealots on this planet. When it comes to politics and religion, the fanatics in either arena will always interpret incidents in a light favorable to themselves, at the expense of the defenseless and uneducated. It is easy for a person in hindsight to construe a world event in a manner to fit his or her belief system, and it is even easier for politicos, priests or government agencies to create history in order to suit themselves or prove their chosen faith, creed or party. Whatever the case, the world suffers for it, because such fabricated and puffed-up renditions of reality are exploitative and repeatedly lead to discord and warfare. There can be no peace on Earth if everything is constantly being viewed through the muddy glasses of belief systems, and belief systems as they apply to "religion" are no

---

[1] Massey, II, 691.
[2] For more on the meaning of Revelation, see my book *The Christ Conspiracy*.

different. It is our destiny to become more universal in our perspectives and behavior, perceiving the cosmos as one, yet filled with utterly unique and marvelous creatures. And *this* prophecy *must* come true, or

we *will* face an apocalyptic nightmare of our own making, the so-called End Times also laid out in the Bible as a blueprint in Revelation that far too many millions of people are enthusiastic about bringing to pass.

# Is Cannibalism a Religious Experience?

This is my body...

"So Jesus said to them, 'Truly, truly, I say to you, unless you eat the flesh of the Son of man and drink his blood, you have no life in you; he who eats my flesh and drinks my blood has eternal life... For my flesh is food indeed, and my blood is drink indeed.'"

John 6:53-55

"From the time of Moses till the time of the prophet Hezekiah, a period of seven hundred years or more, the Hebrews were idolaters, as their records show. The serpent was reverenced as the Healer of the Nation; they worshipped a bull called Apis, as did the Egyptians; they worshipped the sun, moon, stars, and all the hosts of heaven; they worshipped fire, and kept it burning on an altar, as did the Persians and other nations; they worshipped stones, revered an oak-tree, and bowed down to images; they worshipped a virgin mother and child; they worshipped Baal, Moloch, and Chemosh (names given to the sun), and offered up human sacrifices to them, after which, in some instances, they ate the victims."[1]

Sarah Titcomb, *Aryan Sun Myths* (88)

---

[1] Cf. Doane, 107-108.

As repulsive as the notion may seem, it is a fact that "theophagy"—the technical term for the consumption of a god's body and blood—has been considered a religious experience globally for thousands of years. While certain cults/religions may think that they invented the concept of the Eucharist or Holy Communion, and that this "Lord's Supper" has nothing whatsoever to do with cannibalism, the ritual of sacrificing a "god" or "goddess" (proxy) and the sharing of his or her blood and body as a sacrament represents an act found throughout the ancient world. The only thing modern religion has done is to maintain the form of the Eucharist in a symbolic rather than literal sense, and for that perhaps we should be grateful.

## The Eucharist

"He who eats my flesh and drinks my blood abides in me, and I in him," so the alleged founder of Christianity, Jesus Christ, purportedly said (Jn 6:56). It may seem abhorrent to Christians of today that one of their most precious rituals actually has its roots in the cannibalistic sacrifice and consumption of their deity. This origin, however, is the fact.

Far from being a Christian invention, the ritual of the Eucharist—from the Greek ευχαριστεω, meaning "to be thankful"—has been practiced for millennia by various religions, cults and sects around the globe. Beginning thousands of years before the Christian myth was established, an actual human being, acting as a proxy for the deity worshipped, was sacrificed and eaten by the cult's followers. In some cases, more than one person was killed and consumed in this matter. This nauseating

"My Flesh is true food, and my Blood true drink." (John 6:55)

God wants to share His life with us
by uniting us to His Son, Jesus Christ
—not only mentally or spiritually, but completely.

behavior went on throughout the ancient world, and the general words regarding this act—"For my flesh is food indeed, and my blood is drink indeed." (Jn. 6:55)—attributed to Jesus may in fact have been part of the ritual.

### Jewish Ritual Sacrifice

As is evident from the texts of the Old Testament, an animal or animals were often substituted in place of a human for the purpose of a scapegoat, as at Exodus 24:6-8:

> And Moses took half of the blood he threw against the altar. Then he took the book of the covenant, and read it in the hearing of the people; and they said, "All that the LORD has spoken we will do, and we will be obedient." And Moses took the blood and threw it upon the people, and said, "Behold the blood of the covenant which the LORD has made with you in accordance with all these words."

The sanguine Israelite sacrifice is also depicted in detail at Exodus 29:12-21, with the blood being thrown all over the altar, as well as upon various body parts and garments of the priest Aaron and "his sons and his sons..."

There can be little doubt that this violent ritual is at the basis of the peculiar—and pogrom-fomenting—remark attributed to the Jews during Jesus's alleged sacrifice: "His blood be on us and on our children." (Mt 27:25)

Exodus 29:63 continues the bloody description:

> ...and every day you shall offer a bull as a sin offering for atonement. Also you shall offer a sin offering for the altar, when you make atonement for it, and shall anoint it, to consecrate it.

Exodus 30:10 likewise depicts the blood atonement to be made by Aaron on an annual basis, a "sin offering" that is "most holy to the LORD."

And at Leviticus 1:5, we also read:

> Then he shall kill the bull before the LORD; and Aaron's sons the priests shall present the blood, and throw the blood round about against the altar that is at the door of the tent of meeting.[1]

In some cultures, such abundant animal sacrifices replaced the human sacrifice, which came to be viewed as repulsive. Nevertheless, human sacrifice—evidenced in the Old Testament by the story of Abraham and Isaac (Gen 22:2), in the dedication of babies to the Semitic god Molech (Lev 20:2ff), and in the ritual killing of various kings (Jos 8:29; 10:26)—was allegedly practiced by the Jews until the time of the Romans, who sought to put an end to it. In *The Religion of Israel to the Fall of the Jewish State*, Dr. Abraham Kuenen, a professor of Theology at the University of Leyden, remarks:

> In the worship of Molech—as we will assume here and prove afterwards—human sacrifice occupies an important place. But it not unfrequently occurs also in the worship of Jahveh. When Micah introduces one of his contemporaries, a worshipper of Jahveh, speaking thus:
>
> > "Shall I give my first-born for my transgression,
> > The fruit of my body for the sin of my soul?"
>
> it is undoubtedly implied that in his days such a sacrifice was not looked upon as at all unreasonable; the prophet himself has other ideas of what Jahveh

---

[1] See other scriptures throughout Leviticus concerning the blood sacrifice of animals, particularly bulls and goats. Numbers likewise contains instructions for the blood atonement, e.g. at 18 and 19.

requires; but if human sacrifice had been foreign to the service of Israel's god, he could not have mentioned it in this manner....[1]

In this regard, Dr. James DeMeo states:

Puritanical followers of Yahweh also sacrificed humans, a practice which peaked out in the area between 800-700 BCE. According to [Dr. Nigel] Davies, burnt offerings were made of infants in large pits, similar to the method of the Phoenicians, King Manasseh (c. 723 BCE) made human sacrifices, as did the prophet Samuel, and Ahaz (c. 730 BCE) offered up his own children. Others, such as Ezekiel (c. 597 BCE), however, condemned child sacrifice.[2]

Fast forward to Christianity, and we find a specific purpose for creating that religion—which includes the killing of God's own son in order to remove transgressions and sins—to put an end to human sacrifice with the once-for-all sacrifice of Christ. In addition to his suffering on the cross, Jesus offers his body and blood as redemption for man's sins, precisely as had occurred in earlier sacred-king human-sacrifice/scapegoat rituals:

> Now as they were eating, Jesus took bread, and blessed, and broke it, and gave it to the disciples and said, "Take, eat; this is my body." And he took a cup, and when he had given thanks he gave it to them, saying, "Drink of it, all of you; for this is my blood of the covenant, which is poured out for many for the forgiveness of sins. (Mt 26:26)

As we know, in Christianity the theophagous act is now purely symbolic, but it was not always this way in the predecessor religions that contributed to the

---

[1] Kuenen, 237.
[2] DeMeo, 270. See 2 Kings 3:26-27, 16:1-4 and Jer 7:30-31.

formation of the Christian faith. Also, the sacrifice of animals as a religious rite still goes on in various parts of the world, as, indeed, does human sacrifice and cannibalism.

## Cannibalism in the Bible

The fact that cannibalism is a favored act of atonement can be shown in the Old Testament at Deuteronomy 28:53-57, where God exacts his punishment against his stiff-necked chosen people, who have made the fatal mistake of not serving "the Lord your God with joyfulness and gladness of heart" (Deut 28:47). The Lord punishes the Hebrews by causing their enemies to besiege them in all their towns, leaving the chosen to eat their offspring. In this passage, God is so perturbed with his chosen ones that he forces them into starvation so that they have only their children to eat, which they apparently do. The evident motivation for the Lord to compel the Jews to do this bizarre and revolting act is so that they will "fear this glorious and awful name, the Lord your God" (Deut 28:58). If the Jews do not obey the Lord, he will further cause them and their offspring "extraordinary afflictions, afflictions severe and lasting, and sickness grievous and lasting" (Deut 28:59).

All this from the "loving" God of the Bible! And remember, the Hebrews got into this trouble in the first place because they did not serve such an abominable and vile god with joyfulness and gladness of heart! But how could they not know that they were supposed to do that when at Deuteronomy 10:20 they are told to "fear the Lord your God" and at Deuteronomy 11:1 they are to "therefore love the Lord your God." It would seem to civilized human beings that it is impossible to fear and love anything or anyone at the same time, but these are the commandments that the chosen people are supposed to follow or else they will be forced to eat their children.

Or how about the following beautiful story from 2 Kings 6:26-30? After invading Samaria, the Israelites are attacked by the Syrians, such that a famine occurs:

> Now as the king of Israel was passing by upon the wall, a woman cried out to him, saying, "Help, my lord, O king!" And he said, "If the Lord will not help you, whence shall I help you? From the threshing floor, or from the wine press?" And the king asked her, "What is your trouble?" She answered, "This woman said to me, 'Give your son, that we may eat him today, and we will eat my son tomorrow.' So we boiled my son, and ate him. And on the next day I said to her, 'Give your son, that we may eat him'; but she has hidden her son." When the king heard the words of the woman he rent his clothes... And while [Elisha] was still speaking with them, the king came down to him and said, "This trouble is from the Lord!..."

The good Lord is forever playing sadistic games with his chosen people, who always seem to be messing up at his direction, after which he gets to punish them. These examples serve to illustrate how problematic is the notion that there is one entity directing everything and that every event is caused by him. The Israelites' enemies also believed this notion, such that their interpretation of what happened would be equally ethnocentric, with their particular god favoring them in the end. In order to keep up the impression that the Lord is always with them, and could not be with their enemies, despite such horrendous circumstances as desperate famine that causes them to eat their own children, the religiously minded and God-obsessed must continuously come up with reasons for their suffering and with complex remedies and rituals to propitiate the wrathful Lord that utterly evade the issue, which is that they are war-like people who cannot expect but like in return. "An eye for an eye, a tooth for a tooth." "He who lives by the sword shall die by the sword," etc.

As discussed in my book *Suns of God: Krishna, Buddha and Christ Unveiled*, ancient Jews were thus claimed to practice cannibalism, to the extent that they were called "horrible cannibals" by Christian scholar and Irish parliamentarian Edwin King or "Lord Kingsborough" (1795-1837).[1] In *Antiquities of Mexico*, Kingsborough writes:

> In nothing did the Mexicans more resemble the Jews than in the multitude of their sacrifices...

> It was customary amongst the Jews to eat a portion of the flesh of sacrifices, and to burn the rest; and Peter Martyr in allusion to that custom says in the fourth chapter in his fifth Decad, that, "As the Jews sometimes eate [sic] the lambs which were sacrificed by the old law, so do they eat mans [sic] flesh, casting only away the hands, feet, and bowels."[2]

Kingsborough also says:

> All the Spanish authors agree that no suffering from famine could induce the Mexicans, when closely besieged by Cortes, to eat the flesh of their country men who had been killed: whence it must be inferred that they only ate the flesh of sacrificed and devoted victims. The Jews were less able to withstand the torments of hunger.[3]

In support of this contention, Kingsborough cites biblical passages, including 2 Kings 6, as noted above, in which a woman confesses to the king of Israel to have eaten her own son, during a siege by the king of Syria. Kingsborough notes that the woman is Samaritan, i.e., northern Israelite, rather than Judean;

---

[1] Acharya, *SOG*, 275-276.
[2] Kingsborough, VI, 232-233. In a terrible twist of fate, Kingsborough's expensive reproduction of the Mexican codices landed him in debtor's prison, where he died of typhus.
[3] Kingsborough, VI, 311fn.

however, Judeans have also been represented as practicing cannibalism, both in the Bible as at Deut 28:53-57 and Micah 3, as well as by other ancient writers, such as the Greco-Egyptian rhetorician Apion (c. 20 BCE-c. 45 AD/CE) and Roman historian Cassius Dio (c. 165-c. 229 AD/CE).[1] In his *Roman History* (Epitome of Book 68, 32, 1-2), Cassius remarks:

> Meanwhile the Jews in the region of Cyrene had put a certain Andreas at their head, and were destroying both the Romans and the Greeks. They would eat the flesh of their victims, make belts for themselves of their entrails, anoint themselves with their blood and wear their skins for clothing; many they sawed in two, from the head downwards; others they gave to wild beasts, and still others they forced to fight as gladiators. In all two hundred and twenty thousand perished. In Egypt, too, they perpetrated many similar outrages, and in Cyprus, under the leadership of a certain Artemion. There, also, two hundred and forty thousand perished.[2]

Reflecting similar atrocity of an earlier era, Micah 3 represents God chastising the "heads of Jacob" and "rulers of the house of Israel" for flaying and eating his people:

> And I said: Hear, you heads of Jacob and rulers of the house of Israel! Is it not for you to know justice?—you who hate the good and love the evil, who tear the skin from off my people, and their flesh from off their bones; who eat the flesh of my people, and flay their skin from off them, and break their bones in pieces, and chop them up like meat in a kettle, like flesh in a caldron.

Of course, biblical literalists have no place to go with this scripture but to assume that God was saying that the Israelite leaders really had been flaying and eating the chosen ones. From the description, it certainly sounds as if the writer had witnessed such

---

[1] Silberstein, 124; Isaac, 210.
[2] Modrzejewski, 202.

grotesque events firsthand. Since this account is nearly identical to rituals performed in Mexico, such a rite definitely *was* practiced by humans at some point and in some era. It does not surprise us then that this grisly ritual also took place in Palestine. In any case, that the Jewish priesthood committed human sacrifice, as did that of so many other cultures, appears undeniable. As Kingsborough further says:

> We have...the highest authority—that of the Scriptures—for affirming that the Jews did frequently perform human sacrifices...[1]

He then cites Dominican friar Gregorio Garcia's *Origin of the Indians* for scriptural authority regarding Jewish human sacrifice. After discussing the priests of the Aztec god Quetzalcoatl, Kingsborough next states:

> We must further observe that as amongst the Jews it was customary for the priests to flay the victims, and afterwards take their skins—as may be proved from the following texts of Scriptures...[2]

His Lordship proceeds to name 2 Chronicles 20, Leviticus 7 and Numbers 25, the latter of which demonstrates the construction of a charnel house for the heads, much as could be found in Mesoamerica. Kingsborough further describes the Mexican human sacrifice thus:

> The Mexicans were accustomed to break the legs of a crucified person on one of their most solemn festivals, and to leave him to die on the cross.[3]

---

[1] Kingsborough, VIII, 16fn.
[2] Kingsborough, VIII, 16fn.
[3] Kingsborough, VIII, 16fn.

Needless to say, this description closely resembles what was done to crucified persons in Judea, as related in the New Testament (Jn 19:31-32). Several other aspects similar to Christian practices could be found in the Mesoamerican religion, including nunneries and monasteries, as well as religious heads like high priests and popes.[1] The European conquerors of Central America, in fact, were stunned by the comparisons, so much so that they posited that Jews and Christians had already made their way to the Americas long before Columbus. Indeed, the "Lost Tribes of Israel" were located all over the place to explain any advanced civilization the Christian explorers discovered.[2] However, no direct evidence of Jewish or Christian influence has ever been found, and many of the correspondences can be explained by the fact of these religions also possessing universal origins set in astrotheology and nature worship.

Like the Semites, the Mexicans also engaged in theophagy, or god eating; indeed, one such communion occurred at the winter solstice, when the Aztecs, as Sir Dr. James George Frazer (1854-1941) relates, "killed" the god Huitzilipochtli "in effigy," after which they ate him.[3] Presumably, the effigy was a human proxy. Preceding this ceremony, a man-shaped image of the god was created with dough made of assorted seeds and the

---

[1] Léon-Portilla, 96; Lafaye, 164. According to the Spanish Jesuit Father Josephus Acosta (c. 1539-1600), "There were in Peru many Monasteries of Virgins (for there are no other admitted) at the least one in every Province. In these Monasteries there were two sorts of women, one ancient, which they called Mamacomas, for the instruction of the young; and the other was of young Maidens, placed there for a certaine time..." (Purchas, 323.)
[2] See Feder, 176-178.
[3] Frazer (1900), 340.

blood of children.[1] Frazer further relates that, according to the Franciscan monk Sahagun, who was "our best authority on the Aztec religion," another human sacrifice was committed at the vernal equinox, i.e., Easter, the precise time when the archetypical Christian Son of God was allegedly put to death.[2] As it was in so many places, the Mexican Easter ritual was practiced doubtlessly for the purpose of fertility and the resurrection of life during the spring.

## Murderous Biblical Rampages

Of course, the above instances are not the only places in the Bible—which as we know from Christians rates as a book of great moral character that should be taught in all our schools—where the Lord is interested in human sacrifice. Much earlier in the story God tries to blackmail the patriarch Abraham into murdering his own son in order to demonstrate his loyalty and devotion. (Gen 22:2) Naturally, if God were a *person* behaving in this manner, he would be considered a great villain. But, the Lord's ways are mysterious, and we cannot know them, so when he behaves like a tyrant and terrorist, it must be something good.

Yet, the Lord is not satisfied with the sacrifice of animals or mere mortals. Eventually, the world cannot be saved unless God's very own son is brutally abused and crucified, an absurd act that somehow makes sense to an awful lot of people who blithely accept it as being able to redeem their own souls, no matter what heinous deeds they might commit. How this action purportedly taken by one man almost two thousand years ago has anything to do with our souls of today is apparently understood by these folks, who must be very clever indeed to see the connection. And what can be said of such a plan by God to save men's souls? Is this truly the best the creator of this vast and astounding cosmos could come up with, getting

---

[1] Frazer (1963), 568.
[2] Frazer (1998), 608.

himself (as his son) crucified by a bunch of low-tech Roman mortals on a minuscule and dinky orb far off to the side of one of infinite galaxies?

All throughout the Judeo-Christian bible—God's infallible word, remember—the Lord is very interested in punishing, torturing, murdering and pillaging. In fact, it is the mark of a good religious person to take out at least a couple of towns, slaughtering every man, woman and child, and stealing their booty, as Moses and his thugs do in the massacre of the Midianites at Numbers 31, for example.[1] The Lord seems to love exacting retribution for indiscretions made by lowly human beings who could not possibly harm the Creator of the Universe, but somehow these foolish little humans who dare to transgress the Lord's laws are a big threat to the almighty God!

**Moral Behavior of God's "Chosen"**

One shining example of a God-fearing man can be found at Judges 19:22-30, the story of the Levite's concubine. The Levites, one must remember, are the priestly tribe of the chosen people, God's favored sons, and they are rewarded by special privileges.[2] They are also, naturally, exempt from the wars that they may cause "in the Lord's name."[3]

---

[1] See also Joshua 6:24, where, after burning Jericho, the Israelites steal all the gold and silver for the "treasury of the house of the LORD." In 2 Samuel 8:11-12, King David dedicates to the Lord all the spoils he has stolen from the cities he sacked.

[2] Num 35:2ff. See Jenson: "A high status in the hierarchy brings with it great privileges, although [they] are not unlimited. The priests had several sources of income and support, including a sizeable share in the booty and the tithes, although they could not own land (Num 18.20). The Levites were also given sources of income, in addition to cities with their pasture lands." (Jenson, 118.)

[3] Jamieson, 96.

The Levites are the upholders of God's law, and as such they are to be protected and esteemed no matter what. In the story of the Levite's concubine—which must be taken literally because everything in the Bible is literally true—the lowly and base men of the town want to "know" or have sex with the Levite who has just entered into one of the town's more "righteous" homes.

The pious man of the house beseeches the village sodomites not to take the Levite to do "this vile thing" but instead offers his virgin daughter and the Levite's concubine. (Remember, good "God-fearing" men are

allowed to have concubines, i.e., prostitutes—it's all in the name of religion!) Luckily for the daughter, the man has to toss out only the concubine in order to satisfy the wicked men, who are apparently bisexual. The lusty men rape and batter the concubine, who is then left on the righteous doorstep, dead.

When the Levite sees her there, brutally beaten and violated, he compassionately yells, "Get up, let us be going." (Judges 19:28) When the murdered concubine fails to rise, the pious Levite then mercifully throws her upon his ass, returns to the house for a knife, cuts her into 12 pieces and sends her body parts to various destinations in Israel. Now, we cannot take this story as being symbolic because the Word of God is literal fact, so we must assume that the Levite's actions are true and that they are in accordance with the

Lord's wishes, because the Levite is the Lord's earthly representative.

## The "Good" Patriarchs

Other examples of men of high moral character held up to be God-fearing representatives of the Lord on Earth can be found at Genesis 12:13, where Abram tells his wife, Sarai, to lie about being his wife, and at Genesis 20:2, where Abram, now called Abraham for his just actions, himself lies about "Sarah" being his

wife. When Abraham is caught in his fib regarding Sarah not being his wife, he continues the lie and doesn't even bat an eye at the incestuous implications, as he tells the king of Gerar— who, thinking Sarah is Abraham's sister, has nearly had sex with her—that Sarah is both his wife *and* his sister, but not by the

same father. The pious prophet's son Isaac also learned his father's trick of lying about his wife being his sister, and he too plays it upon the king of Gerar at Genesis 26:7. The king finds him out when he catches Isaac fondling his wife, but Isaac, not as good a liar as his papa, tells him the truth. For his high moral character, Isaac is eventually made very wealthy by the Lord.

In addition, at Genesis 16:3, Abram commits adultery and bigamy with Hagar the Egyptian (not to mention treason, since Egypt was an enemy of the Lord's chosen). Remember, this example represents the godly behavior of one of the Lord's greatest prophets.

As John E. Remsburg says:

Who was Abraham? An insane barbarian patriarch who married his sister, denied his wife, and seduced her handmaid; who drove one child into the desert to starve, and made preparations to butcher the other.[1]

Of course, Abraham is not the only pious person who displays behavior which would be unacceptable by today's moral standards but which is considered perfectly fine and virtuous because it is committed by a biblical character. At Genesis 20:32-36, the divinely chosen Lot is made drunk and then seduced by his daughters. This immoral act is done, one assumes, with the blessings of the Lord, because it serves to continue the Hebraic lineage. One wonders why the all-powerful God could not find an alternative to this incestuous reproduction for his chosen.

The list of impious behavior by biblical "heroes" and exemplars of the Lord's will goes on:[2]

Noah gets plastered and exposes himself. (Gen 9:20-23)

King David also vulgarly exposes himself to a crowd. (2 Sam 6:20)

David possibly has a love affair with Jonathan. (1 Sam 18-20)

"Wise" and "moral" King Solomon has "seven hundred wives, princesses, and three hundred concubines." (1 Ki 11:3)

Concerning various biblical characters, Remsburg further remarks:

> Who was Jacob? Another patriarch, who won God's love by deceiving his father, cheating his uncle, robbing his brother, practicing bigamy with two of his cousins, and committing fornication with two of his housemaids.

> Who was Moses? A model of meekness; a man who boasted of his own humility; a man who murdered an Egyptian and hid his body in the sand; a man who exterminated whole nations to secure the spoils of war, a man who butchered in cold blood

---

[1] Leedom, 113. Reprinted from Remsburg's *Bible Morals*, Truth Seeker, 1905.
[2] With acknowledgment to Akerley's *The X-Rated Bible*.

thousands of captive widows; a man who tore dimpled babes from the breasts of dying mothers and put them to a cruel death; a man who made orphans of thirty-two thousand innocent girls, and turned sixteen thousand of them over to the brutal lusts of a savage soldiery.

Who was David? "A man after God's own heart." A vulgar braggadocio, using language to a woman the mere quoting of which would send me to prison; a traitor, desiring to lead an enemy's troops against his own countrymen; a thief and robber, plundering the country on every side; a liar, uttering wholesale falsehoods to screen himself from justice; a red-handed butcher, torturing and slaughtering thousands of men, women, and children, making them pass through burning brick-kilns, carving them up with saws and axes, and tearing them into pieces under harrows of iron [2 Sam 12:31]; a polygamist, with a harem of wives and concubines; a drunken debauchee, dancing half-naked before the maids of his household;

a lecherous old libertine, abducting and ravishing the wife of a faithful soldier; a murderer, having his faithful soldier put to death after desolating his home; a hoary-headed fiend, foaming with vengeance on his dying bed, demanding with his last breath the deaths of two aged men, one of whom had most contributed to make his kingdom what it was, the other a man to whom he had promised protection.[1]

And so on and so on throughout the "Holy" Bible. (Which should be taught in every school but definitely wouldn't make it to our movies screens or would be V-chipped out of our TVs.) In light of this analysis, it is

---

[1] Leedom, 113.

difficult to believe that God would send his messiah and "gentle Son" through the house and lineage of the murderous and brutal King David! (Mt 1:1)

## What Does God Do with All the Foreskins?

What to make of the obsession with the foreskin and circumcision found within the pages of "God's Word?" In the Old Testament, in order to please his

future father-in-law, King David enthusiastically abides by the man's request that the monarch slay 100 hundred Philistines and bring the father-in-law their foreskins in exchange for the hand of his daughter! (1 Sam 27) Indeed, the eager David brings Saul

*200* foreskins! In the New Testament, circumcision is dwelt upon repeatedly by Paul and others, so critical is it to the Lord, who obviously messed up in the first place by putting foreskins on men.

## The Good Book—Does it Produce Morality?

Cannibalism, rape, mutilation, murder—these are never-ending themes of the book that "should be taught in every school" and that forms the moral basis of many societies. What is going on here?

Considering that the Lord seems well pleased with wars and massacres; rape; theft; deceit; trickery; adultery; cruelty to men, women, children and animals; tyranny; murder; and cannibalism, it is surprising that those who engage in such behavior today are not rewarded for it but are actually punished—at least in the Western world. No doubt Charles Manson and other murderers were taught the "Good Book" in Sunday school and were

MANSON, Charles Milles

CII 966 856

just acting it out. As Dr. Harold Schechter says:

> Some of the most monstrous killers in American
> history were religious fanatics who could recite
> Scripture from memory and—when they weren't
> busy torturing children or mutilating corpses—loved
> to do nothing better than read the Good Book.[1]

## Is the New Testament Exempt from Moral Turpitude?

But wait, some may say, that is the *Old* Testament.
The *New* Testament reveals a *loving* God. So, we might
respond, the "infallible" God changes halfway through
the story? Perhaps he got sick of himself and decided
to reform his evil ways? In actuality, the atrocities of
the New Testament are plentiful for a relatively short
text, such as constant exhortations for slaves to obey
their masters in all ways (Eph 6:5; Col 3:22; Tit 2:9),
followers to castrate themselves for the Lord (Mt
19:12), or women to be submissive to their husbands
(Eph 5:22, 24; Col 3:18), etc. How about the whole
concept of cannibalistic ritual somehow being
"spiritual" or that the torture and crucifixion of a
"scapegod" somehow redeems the rest of us?

The notion of the Eucharist as real cannibalism
unfortunately has occurred to a number of individuals
over the centuries, including the heinous child-
murderer Albert Fish, who told a psychiatrist after he
dismembered and ate a 12-year-old girl that he
"associated the eating of the
child's flesh and the drinking of
her blood with the 'idea of Holy
Communion.'"[2] Fish was a
religious fanatic who also
believed that his repeated child-
murder was ordained from on
high, as in the story of Abraham.
In justifying his despicable deeds,
Fish cited the passage at Psalms

---

[1] Schechter, 333.
[2] Schechter, 333-334.

137:9: "Happy shall he be who takes your little ones and dashes them against the rock!"

No matter how far away from it we wish to get, theophagy used to signify the actual dismemberment and consumption of a human being, and the Eucharist was a cannibalistic act, plain and simple. Just remember that fact every time you go to church and drink that wine and eat that bread.

In the end, don't believe us—read your Bible! If you can stomach it.... Be sure to check with your pastor first, though, to make sure it's got a G rating.

# What is a Cult?

"What is a cult? *A cult is someone else's religious group that does not agree with mine.* That may be a light-hearted definition, but it does have a ring of truth to it. Because religion is so personalized it is often difficult to objectively sort out what is true and what is false. There are many variable factors to consider in determining whether a religious group ought to be categorized as a cult, a fundamentalist fringe movement, a sect, a denomination, or an entirely different world religious tradition, and there are unavoidable inconsistencies...."

Dr. Ruth A. Tucker, *Another Gospel: Cults, Alternative Religions, and the New Age Movement* (15)

Over the centuries, many religious movements have cropped up that have been dismissed as "cults." But, what is a cult? And what makes it different from a religion? Is it simply a question of size or longevity? Is not a religion a cult when it first starts, slowly becoming a religion as it ages and gains followers? And cannot just about any organization—even those not deemed "religious" *per se*—be considered a cult?

## The Definition of Cult

What is a cult? A cult, as defined by Merriam-Webster's, is:

1. formal religious veneration; 2. a religious system; also its adherents; 3. faddish devotion; also a group of persons showing such devotion.[1]

Others define it thus:

Cult (totalist type): a group or movement exhibiting a great or excessive devotion or dedication to some person, idea, or thing, and employing unethical, manipulative or coercive techniques of persuasion and control (e.g., isolation from former friends and family, debilitation, use of special methods to heighten suggestibility and subservience, powerful group pressures, information management, promotion of total dependency on the group and fear of leaving it, suspension of individuality and critical judgment, etc.), designed to advance the goals of the group's leaders, to the possible or actual detriment of members, their families, or the community. (DJ West, 1989)[2]

Another cult expert, Dr. Margaret T. Singer, writes:

I classify cults into nine different types:

—those based on neo-Christianity ideas;
—those based on Hindu and Eastern concepts;
—those based on the occult involving witchcraft and Satanism;
—those based on spiritualism;
—those based on Zen and other sino-Japanese practices;
—those based on race;
—those involving flying saucer and other outer space phenomena;
—those involving psychology; and
—political cults.[3]

Gee, there's no cult-ural bias here!

Next we have commentary from the National Association for the Advancement of Psychoanalysis:

[1] Merriam-Webster, 192.
[2] See, e.g., Lynn, 271.
[3] Reed, 214.

When do cults arise? Throughout history, whenever there has been a breakdown in the structure of the society, an uprise in cults has occurred. For example, after the French Revolution, there was a tremendous upsurge of cults in France and in Europe; when the Industrial Revolution came to England, many cults arose. In the United States the westward frontier expansion and the growth of cults occurred together.

What is a cult? It is a group led by a living, self-proclaimed leader who claims that he or she has been told by a higher power to lead such a group. Secondly, cults have a double set of ethics, that is, one set of rules for use in the cult, and another for use with non-members. Thirdly, cults raise funds for their own use and not for altruistic purposes.[1]

Let us now use the various criteria presented above to evaluate some groups not usually perceived as "cults" by most people. The Catholic Church is self-explanatory, while "IRS" refers to the American tax collection agency, the Internal Revenue Service, and "CIA" is the American spook organization called the Central Intelligence Agency.

| Cult Characteristics | Catholic Church | IRS | CIA |
|---|---|---|---|
| Formal religious veneration | X | ? | ? |
| A religious system | X | ? | ? |
| Faddish devotion | X | X | X |
| A group of persons showing such devotion | X | X | X |
| A group or movement exhibiting a great or | | | |

---

[1] NAAP Journal, vol. 9/no. 4, "Socio and Religious Cults: Religion or Brainwashing?"

| | | | |
|---|---|---|---|
| excessive devotion or dedication to some person, idea, or thing | X | X | X |
| Employing unethical, manipulative or coercive techniques of persuasion and control | X | X | X |
| Isolation from former friends and family | X | X | X |
| Debilitation | X | X | X |
| Use of special methods to heighten suggestibility and subservience | X | X | X |
| Powerful group pressures | X | X | X |
| Information management | X | X | X |
| Promotion of total dependency on the group and fear of leaving it | X | X | X |
| Suspension of individuality and critical judgment | X | X | X |
| Designed to advance the goals of the group's leaders, to the possible or actual detriment of members, their families, or the community | X | X | X |
| Double set of ethics | X | X | X |
| Raising funds for own benefit | X | X | X |

**Governmental Bodies Guilty of "Religious Veneration?"**

Some will ask, "How can you suggest that the IRS and CIA are formal religious veneration?" Webster's defines "religious" as "relating or devoted to the divine or that which is held to be of ultimate importance."

Keep in mind that many people find money to be of ultimate importance and the acquisition of it to be a "divine pursuit." Many secular and sacred institutions are obsessed with raising loads of capital—no matter what it takes. They are often members of the "money cult."

"To venerate" is defined as "to regard with reverential respect." Certainly by any standards or applications there are many within these systems who are zealots for the party line. So it has always been throughout history. These secular organizations can be cliques, factions and, yes, cults. In order for these groups to function, there often must a binding factor and a perceived enemy. The CIA, for instance, purportedly has served at times as a sophisticated brainwashing system that has contributed to civil unrest and degradation globally. The IRS *religiously* persecutes those in its path, strong and weak alike, and reduces us to robotoid status under its everwatching and ready-to-strike eyes.[1] Each group has its particular mass psyche, its shared goals and beliefs. Each holds said vision as of ultimate importance and regards the mission and members with reverential respect.

## The Catholic Church is a Bigger Cult than the Moonies

That the Catholic Church is a formal religious veneration goes without saying. It is certainly a faddish devotion when one considers that it has only occupied a fraction of human history and represents one of thousands of godmen/ hero myths found globally.

---

[1] This essay was composed during the 1990s, when the IRS was notoriously at the height of its power. It has since been "reformed" in order to address abuses and excesses. Yet, there remain many horror stories of broken people and families being destroyed by governmentally induced or exacerbated hardship.

Without a doubt the Church is guilty of excessive devotion to a person, idea or thing, and it certainly is "a group led by a living leader who claims that he or she has been told by a higher power to lead such a group." The minds of devout Catholics are constantly obsessed with the "Lord and Savior" and "God the Father," among other religious ideas and artifacts. To a Catholic, all revolves around the "Lord's plan" or some other such notion. Everything is perceived from this theocentric platform, as it is also in Christianity in general, as well as Judaism and Islam. In fact, throughout Catholicism's sordid and shameful past, those who did not share this perception have been hideously scourged, tortured, burned at the stake, massacred, robbed and made victims of other unlovely deeds perpetrated against them by "good Christians." The obsession with the "Kingdom of Heaven" and the "Kingdom of the Lord" led to deaths of millions, during the inquisitions, crusades and other Christian exploits worldwide.

## Mainstream Groups Use Cultlike Brainwashing Techniques

The IRS and CIA are also single-focused in their pursuits, so much so that they have allegedly broken laws, both nationally and internationally. This lawbreaking has purportedly led to the harassment and death of thousands as well. The IRS has been accused of using mind control techniques at times to produce illness in people it perceives owe it money. At times its agents have been  relentless and uncaring, as if from some other species. They appear to care not a fig about hardship, but go after the "little people" who are barely scraping buy, while they frequently appear above the law. The CIA's alleged escapades internationally are infamous. Their espionage and mental harassment techniques rank as state of the art, and they seem to capitulate to almost nothing. Their "missions" are of the highest importance, and they are excessively devoted to them.

The techniques of coercion used by any of these groups are also well known. While the IRS and CIA are slightly more surreptitious than the Catholics, the Church flagrantly has used physical and psychological torture to persuade "heathens" and other "sinners" to repent or convert. Priests have been alleged to quip, "Give me a child before the age of seven, and he's mine for life."[1] All religions have "brainwashing" techniques as part of their curricula. The very doctrines of Catholicism are coercive: Obey, and you will be rewarded; disobey, and you will be punished. You are offered greed for heaven or fear of hell.

Likewise, the IRS uses high-stress techniques by way of threats to one's livelihood and sometimes one's life. The stress associated with finance and the pressures put on by IRS hassles can be very great indeed. There is virtually no American over the age of 22 who is free from these pressures, not even the rich, although they may be insulated from it. These are some of the highest stresses in the world, and there have been cases reported of people harassed by the IRS going insane, committing suicide or being killed in combats with this agency. This harassment has included rumors of the use of mind-control weapons such as those reportedly also employed by the CIA.

The CIA uses its coercive techniques in a more subtle and hidden manner, although its various operations also reveal the propensity for physical and psychological torture as well. It has been accused of turning a blind eye and deaf ear to sinister operations in countries in which it has worked, and

---

[1] A longer variant: "Give me a child until he is seven years old and I will give him back to the world, and he will always be a Catholic." (*Herald of Gospel Liberty*, 303.)

it has been linked over the last several decades to illicit drug and weapons deals.[1] The CIA has been rumored to have used such things as electromagnetic waves and drugs to alter or "brain-dirty" subjects.

## Isolate and Conquer

How the Catholic Church isolates people from their

families is obvious when one looks at their principal places of religious training: monasteries and nunneries. These institutions often require a more or less strict renunciation of all that is outside the walls of the compound and a surrender to constant contemplation on the nebulous father-figure in the sky and his son. Depending on the location, the isolation may be total and for many years. The difference between this and other cults is that when the disgruntled or disturbed members of the others escape and reveal the inner workings, we are shocked, while those who have not benefited but may have actually become depraved from the confinement of the monastery are seldom allowed to reach the media. Moreover, until recently the Church has been immensely capable of downplaying or denying the many charges of child molestation and rape by multitudes of "good fathers." If the "population, family and friends" from whom a person is separated are not of the same cult as Catholicism, the isolation may be for a very long time. This segregation happens in every family where an offspring may decide to change his or her religion from what is perceived by the family as "the real one," which means their own. Christianity also has as one of its tenets laid down by its supposed founder that you must "hate your mother and father" to follow its leader. Indeed, Jesus calls for renunciation of the family, as at Luke 14:26:

---

[1] See "Coverup," narrated by Elizabeth Montgomery.

"If any one comes to me and does not hate his own father and mother and wife and children and brothers and sisters, yes, and even his own life, he cannot be my disciple."[1]

In preaching the party line, the IRS and CIA all require their members to appear for many hours a day away from their families, at the office or out on assignment. IRS agents must be one of the most isolated groups around. And what kind of stress are they under, to be compelled constantly to believe that many people are deadbeats who need correction by their organization? This last criterion of social isolation is one shared by all the cults we are dealing with herein.

The debilitation of all of these groups happens not only to their members but also to the outside people the group affects. The debilitation of Church members lies in the "born-in-sin" ideology of the Church and the separation of the divine from the human consciousness. In believing that they are lesser beings, Catholics are set up as victims of existence, which is dictated by the caprice of their often wrathful god.

## Rome Fiddles While the World Burns

The second and third definitions previously cited, to wit—"Secondly, cults have a double set of ethics, that is, one set of rules for use in the cult, and another for use with non-members" and "Thirdly, cults raise funds for their own use and not for altruistic purposes"—could easily be applied to Christian, Jewish or Muslim organizations, including the Catholic Church, whose members exploited, raped, enslaved and impoverished millions of people

---

[1] This quote is from the Revised Standard Version of the New Testament. Some apologists attempt to argue that what Jesus really meant was that "you must love" Jesus more than your parents, etc. However, even the NLT version from which this diluted translation comes has a footnote that reads "Greek *you must hate*." The original Greek word is μισεω or *miseo*, which means "to *hate*," as in "misogyny" and "misanthrope."

worldwide while handing out token "charity." How much pilfered wealth does the Vatican contain, while people around the globe starve?

Cult is also defined as, "A religious sect generally construed to be extremist or bogus." For centuries there have been very vocal detractors of the Catholic Church, including those who have regularly claimed the pope to be the Antichrist.[1] The same arguments relegating them to the status of "cult" could be and have been made as concerns all of the major religions.

### "Cult" is Often Simply Name-Calling

While various organizations, whether religious or otherwise, can be considered as "cults," regardless of their size, function or purported respectability, this analysis serves also to demonstrate that the term "cult" could be used as a pejorative that is frequently slung at groups which fall outside mainstream beliefs as well. In this regard, the "nine different types" of cults as proposed by Dr. Singer constitute culturally biased criteria. The fact is that a number of these "nine types" have been on this planet in one form or another for as long or longer than the relatively recently created Christianity. Mainstream religions were also created during a "break down in the structure of society." By Singer's definition of a cult as a "group led by a living self-proclaimed leader who claims that he or she has been told by a higher power to lead such a group"—or who is essentially viewed as a "divine incarnation" of some sort—early Judaism, Hinduism, Buddhism, Christianity and Islam must be considered cults, if we accept Moses, Krishna, Buddha, Jesus and Mohammed as historical figures. Therefore, by this definition, a cult becomes a religion after its founder is dead. Hence, all religions with founders begin as cults.

---

[1] See, e.g, *A Candid Examination of the Question Whether the Pope of Rome is the Great Antichrist of Scripture* by Rev. Dr. John Henry Hopkins, Bishop of Vermont.

Using the criteria presented in this treatise, we can categorize virtually any group of individuals with shared ideology as a cult, and that includes all religions and organizations known to mankind. Let's keep that fact in mind next time someone starts shouting, "Cult! Cult!" He or she may be a cult unto him or herself.

# Is God a Transsexual?

"Thou Sun Goddess of Arinna art an honored deity; Thy name is held high among names; Thy divinity is held high among the deities; Nay, among the deities, Thou alone O Sun Goddess art honored; Great art Thou alone O Sun Goddess of Arinna; Nay compared to Thee no other deity is as honored or great..."[1]

> Hymn from the 15th Century BCE, found at Bohazköy, Turkey

"In Neolithic periods in Anatolia, the Great Goddess was extolled. Her worship appeared in the shrines of Catal Hüyük of 6500 BC."

> Merlin Stone, *When God was a Woman* (44)

At first glance, the very question looks blasphemous to the pious religious person: Is God a transsexual? The religionist in this day and age often thinks he or she is religious for the reason that he or she believes in a *male* god who has purportedly been described and recorded in one particular book or another which the religious individual is taught to believe was also written or dictated by that very god person himself. The fact that simply following a book or its priests, or merely believing in an anthropomorphic god, does not necessarily make a person religious is not the subject of this particular treatise. However, this fact does need to be pointed out here, because religious people erroneously believe that sheepishly and blindly going

---

[1] Stone, x.

along with a prescribed faith and not questioning "authority" *is* a religious experience, while those who are doubters and nonfollowers are considered either irreligious, atheistic or "satanic."

## Believers are No More Religious than Nonbelievers

The term "religious" comes from the Latin word *religiōsus*, which in turn is derived from *religiō*, meaning: "supernatural constraint/taboo; obligation; sanction; worship; rite; sanctity; reverence/ respect/awe/conscience/scruples; religion."[1] Since scrupulousness and conscientiousness are considered marks of being "religious," it is therefore not necessarily true that individuals who believe in a specific description of God are religious while those who do not believe are not religious. In this sense, a person who does not believe in a god can be and often is *more* "religious"—i.e., diligently scrupulous and conscientious—than an individual who does believe in God, as *many nonbelievers have frequently done outstanding humanitarian work*, demonstrating a true moral character, which should be the mark of religiosity if such a term is to have any meaning at all. In the meantime, throughout history there have been innumerable actions taken by "religious" people that could only be considered horrendous and atrocious criminal behavior. It is quite apparent that few people have ever waged a war *in the name* of atheism. Many, if not most, wars have been fought in the name of one god or another.

Theists hold up Communism and Nazism, along with the regime of the Cambodian tyrant Pol Pot, as evidence of murderous "atheist" tyrannies that have caused the deaths of tens of millions. While it may be true that Communism portrayed itself as "godless," it did not wage war *in the name* of atheism, nor were its founders and leaders raised as atheists. They were, in fact, preponderantly Jewish and Christian. *Communist*

---

[1] www.archives.nd.edu/cgi-bin/words.exe?religio

*Manifesto* writer Karl Marx was born a Jew, the grandson of two rabbis,[1] and was converted to Christianity at age 6.[2] Leon Trotsky, whose real name was Lev Bronstein, was born and raised a Jew but later declared himself "an internationalist."[3]

Josef Stalin's "very religious" mother named him after St. Joseph,[4] and wanted him to become a priest.[5] Stalin himself supposedly claimed that his father had been a priest,[6] and he was purportedly "damaged by violence" while being "raised in a poor priest-ridden household."[7] As a youth, Stalin spent five years in a Greek Orthodox seminary,[8] after which he purportedly renounced his religion. In his later years, Stalin apparently embraced Christianity once more. As Stalin biographer Edvard Radinsky remarks, "During his mysterious retreat [of June 1941] the ex-seminarist had decided to involve the aid of the God he had rejected."[9] Radinsky likewise chronicles a number of religious comrades in Stalin's immediate circle. It is evident that, whether for good or bad, religion played a significant role in Stalin's life.

Adolf Hitler was raised a Catholic, and in a speech in 1922 he remarked, "My feeling as a Christian points me to my Lord and Saviour as a fighter...."[10] In his autobiography *Mein Kampf* (1.2), Hitler stated:

> Hence today I believe that I am acting in accordance with the will of the Almighty Creator: by defending

---

[1] Manuel, 4; Wheen, 9.
[2] Telushkin, 269.
[3] Telushkin, 269; Dasgupta, 113.
[4] Haugen, 15.
[5] Montefiore, 26.
[6] Montefiore, 26.
[7] Montefiore, 27.
[8] Lyons, 40.
[9] Radinsky, 472.
[10] Dawkins, 275.

myself against the Jew, I am fighting for the work of the Lord.[1]

Throughout his life, Hitler invoked God and "the Lord," demonstrating his *religious*, not atheistic, nature.

Pol Pot was raised a Buddhist and Catholic.[2] In this regard, Dr. Ian Harris, a Reader in Religious Studies at the University College of St. Martin, relates: "In one of his early writings Pol Pot wrote approvingly that the 'democratic regime will bring back the Buddhist moralism because our great leader Buddha was the first to have taught [democracy].'"[3] Although in comparison to the Abrahamic religions its history is far less violent, Buddhism has not been entirely devoid of atrocity in its spread and practice.[4]

All combined, hundreds of millions of people have been murdered by "good Christians," "pious Muslims," "humble Jews," "devout Hindus," "practicing Buddhists" and so on. Even if the war has not been specifically declared a "religious" one, we can be certain that the vast majority of the leaders and the troops believe they are fighting a "just cause" with God on their side.

The above assertion serves simply to establish that merely believing in a particular god does not automatically make a person religious and conscientious, while not believing in a god does not make one irreverent and unscrupulous. Questioning the beliefs of others and being a scientist also does not make one irreligious. It is the right of every individual to question any dogma or doctrine regarding what is held to be a very important issue, i.e., religion and the

---

[1] Dawkins, 275.
[2] Frankel, 271.
[3] Harris, 65.
[4] See, e.g., the history of Buddhism imposed upon Tibet and the persecution of Bonpo priests there in the 8th century AD/CE. (Rockhill, 219; McKay, 505.) See also DeMeo about the Buddhist arrival in Japan: "Young girls and boys were procured to meet the sexual demands of the Buddhist clergy inside the temples..." (DeMeo, 356.) Another source is Levy's *Sex, Love and the Japanese*.

nature of God. It is incumbent upon each person to
determine the truth and not blindly believe in others'
opinions in this matter—in fact, this *quest for truth* is
what determines religiosity.

So, in asking the question, "Is God a transsexual?"
we are not being irreligious at all. In reality, it takes a
very religious person—i.e., one who is extremely
dedicated to uncovering the truth about spiritual
matters—even to come up with such a question. If we
are sincerely interested in knowing what is the
Ultimate Truth—that which we could call "God"—we
need to study this subject fervently and not just
accept dogma as a matter of "faith." In studying this
subject, then, we will discover that for the past 2,500
years or so the predominant depiction of the Ineffable
has been as a male, but if we *religiously* delve further
into the issue, we will realize that over the millennia
humanity has created a plethora of portrayals of God,
including a very long period when "God" was perceived
as being *female*.

## When God was a Woman

The fact is that during a large part of human
existence God was viewed as a woman. This

fact means that before
the exclusive domination
of a monotheistic male
god, much of the world
recognized and worshipped
a female version for
thousands of years—longer
than society has depicted
the male version as
dominant. The male interpretation of God is not new,
but its emphasis and totality *are* relatively recent.
Most folks are taught that the ancient world was
totally confused, unenlightened and ignorant of the
existence of the male god now presented in sacred
scriptures, until a particular prophet or son of God
came along to enlighten all these stupid and perplexed

people. While this version of reality has been extraordinarily profitable for those who have perpetuated it, it remains untrue. Many ancient people had an excellent grip on reality and had divined much if not all of what is now contained in the supposed "revelations" called the Bible or Koran long before the prophets and son of God ever purportedly appeared on the planet. The ancients had their male gods and sons, as well as their female goddesses and daughters. Again, what is new is the exclusive domination of the male.

### Nothing New Under the Sun

Although they are depicted as being new and revolutionary, the reality is that a number of the most significant ideas and sayings attributed to esteemed religious thinkers or prophets, whether Jewish, Muslim, Christian or Buddhist, were already in existence well before these figures supposedly brought them to light. In actuality, numerous cultures had recorded nearly the identical "divine" concepts eons earlier in various places around the world, such as Egypt and India. In other words, there is little new or revelatory about major concepts in the Judeo-Christian bible or its offshoot scriptures developed later, the Koran.

In this same regard, for thousands of years conscious and aware peoples around the globe recognized and worshipped a female version of God, the Goddess, and their belief in and acknowledgment of this goddess were just as divinely inspired and truthful as the belief in and acknowledgment of the presently accepted version of God. The people who recognized this female deity were not a bunch of ignorant and illiterate cavemen who simply did not know better. As stated, these folks had recorded the same "sublime" notions found in later scriptures; therefore, they were obviously no less illuminated. The worshippers of the Goddess were as evolved and intelligent as the creators of the male God and "his Word." Indeed, in many parts of the world, the Goddess-worshipping cultures were *more* civilized and enlightened than their successors and conquerors, those of the warrior God-worshipping cultures.

### No Proof that "Great Spirit" is a Man

To ancient believers, the Goddess was just as concrete a reality as the male god is to the believers of today, and they would be just as able to argue intelligently the case for the existence of Goddess as  are the proponents of God able to debate this issue today. One of the arguments the male God-believers throw up to those who question their interpretation of the nature of God is, "The Bible says so" or "The Koran says so." In other words, if you ask a believer in the currently accepted depiction of God how he or she knows that God is a male or that the angels are all male, he or she may reply, "Because the Bible/Koran says so." Needless to say, to a nonbeliever in the biblical/ koranic view of reality, that is like saying, "I believe Elvis is alive because the tabloids say so." A book which seeks to prove its own premises by stating that they are true because the book itself says so, is not a great reference to use. Every criminal is also innocent because he says so—are we to act strictly on his word? Obviously, blind belief is hardly a scientific endeavor.

Since there is in reality no proof that God is a male, and since millions of intelligent people over the millennia have also believed in Goddess, it would seem that this matter is open to debate. And if the overwhelmingly accepted interpretation of the Creator of the Universe was, for thousands of years preceding the domination of the male version, a female, that would leave one to wonder if God has had a sex-change operation. God was once Goddess. When the

Goddess reigned, she was as real as the God is today. Since Goddess was real before God became dominant, we have to wonder if God is a transsexual. What else could it be?

While this question ranks as merely tongue in cheek, the issues raised here remain significant. It is important that every individual blindly willing to go marching off to kill other people because the leaders have deemed the cause "just"—whether for reasons of "religion," "democracy" or some other such thing— know the facts before he or she makes the decision to murder his or her fellow human being. People who believe in things other than what is in your holy scriptures or than the presently accepted rendition of God are *not* evil beings who deserve to die. They are every bit as human as you are, and you have no right or cause to end their lives simply because they do not accept your interpretation of morality or the nature of God as dictated by your "scriptures." Do not listen to your political and religious leaders as they foam at the mouth telling you that this group of people is evil and needs to be corrected simply because their god or goddess has a different face than yours. Explore this issue. Become educated to the fact that "God" has taken on numerous forms and shapes, including female ones, for thousands of years. The nature of the Divine is completely open to interpretation, and no priest or politician has the total picture or the right to act in God's name. There exists also the concept of "No God," i.e., that there is no such creature, separate and apart from creation.

### "Holy War" is Not Holy

If based purely on faith, no religious war is just. All are attempts to force others' opinions of the Divine on "infidels," "heathens" and "pagans." The wars are justified in the name of God or some political system with God at the helm, but the real motives are often territorial, economical or simply bloodlust. Do not be a part of this atrocity, no matter how much someone exhorts you. See through their game, knowing that the Divine cannot be described or contained in a single book, whether Jewish-biased, Christian-biased, Arab-biased or Chinese-biased. Do not kill anyone because they do not share your own ethnocentric and egocentric biases.

## THOU SHALT NOT KILL

Murdering someone in the name of your particular interpretation of God is *not* religious and will absolutely, positively *not* get you into Heaven. On the contrary, when you eventually become enlightened and develop a conscience, your actions will propel you into a "mind *hell*" of your own creation. You will have to live with your actions and replay them over and over again in your mind. Your  actions will come back to haunt and torture you. You will have to find a way to reconcile yourself to the fact that you may have murdered a completely innocent person or persons—all because someone else convinced you that you were acting justly in vindication of some utterly arbitrary interpretation of God. You do not want to live with that evil on your conscience. Do not go along with this type of behavior. Remember that God and religion are subjective and whimsical. Nothing that has form, whether male or female, black or white, represents the ultimate truth. To fight for the real "God" would be to fight for the absolute truth, which in turn is to not fight at all.[1]

---

[1] I am not a pacifist under all circumstances. If someone attacks me, my family or friends, I will respond—with words, legal actions and physical self-defense, if necessary. In this text, I am attempting to inspire people to *fight* for their hard-earned freedoms. Nevertheless, this essay serves to illustrate the reprehensibility of murdering others in the name of God and religion, as engaged in by religious fanatics and maniacs over the past several thousand years.

# Abusing Women is Not Religion

"In the older code in [Deuteronomy], women are generally viewed as...a property of their fathers and then of their husbands. This property-character of a woman is spelled out specifically in terms of her sexual qualities.... In the [Deuteronomy Sex Texts] women are rarely referred to as persons or agents in their own right..."

Rev. Dr. J. Harold Ellens, *Sex in the Bible* (69)

"...the women should keep silence in the churches. For they are not permitted to speak, but should be subordinate, as even the law says."

1 Corinthians 4:34

"Let a woman learn in silence with all submissiveness. I permit no woman to teach or to have authority over men; she is to keep silent."

1 Timothy 2:11-12

"Likewise you wives, be submissive to your husbands..."

1 Peter 3:1

"Men have authority over women because God has made the one superior to the other... Good women are obedient. As for those from whom you fear disobedience, admonish them, forsake them in beds apart, and beat them."[1]

Koran/Quran 4:34

There are certain individuals on this planet of appalling dementia who believe that subjugating, enslaving and torturing human beings who happen to be in female bodies has something to do with "religion." These disturbed individuals justify their despicable and disgusting behavior by claiming it to be laid down by some god monster who is somehow pleased by this wanton abuse of "his" creatures. In addition to the pervasive and hideous brainwashing and psychological, spiritual and emotional abuse forced upon women that they are "inferior" and must serve basically as servants and slaves to their husband-masters, a number of cultures somehow find it "godly" or "righteous" to torture women physically by covering them up, depriving them of life-giving sunlight and subjecting them to grueling heat, among assorted other ghastly torments.

## "Religions" Represent Mental, Emotional and Spiritual Torture

In nations under the domination of the Judeo-Christian-Islamic/Abrahamic conditioning, many millions of women have been taught that they hold no authority and must submit themselves to their father, husband, priest, imam or a giant male god in the sky who is looming and lording over them at all times. This subjugation is authorized, naturally, by that god person's "holy" scriptures, as in: "... the head of a woman is her husband," etc. For the basic attitude towards women in Christianity, for example, let us quote the Christian apostle Paul, whose mind has had such an influence upon the Western world: "It is well for a man not to touch a woman." (1 Cor 7:1)

---

[1] Dawood (1990), 64.

Of course, this sentiment is somewhat milder than the Old Testament attitude towards Woman, which is that she created the sinful state of mankind and must thereafter be punished—for eternity, no less!—by the "merciful" Lord. If a woman commits this or that so-called transgression according to biblical "morals," she is to be stoned or suffer some other bloody fate. And let us not forget that orthodox Jews start their joyful day by thanking God for not making them a woman![1] The female oppression in ultra-orthodox Jewish sects includes: arranged marriages; the shaving of married women's heads and wearing of a wig or *sheitel*; and the daily testing for menstrual blood (*bedikot*), which is considered *niddah*, a Hebrew term often translated as "impure" or "filthy."[2]

We must also address the oppression of women in Islam as well, as demonstrated abundantly by the way in which they are treated on a daily basis all over the Muslim world and increasingly in the West as well. As it says in the Koran (4:34):

---

[1] Jackson, N., 423.

[2] Howland, 37; Siegel, 318; Wasserfall, 234. See also Eisenberg: "Judaism prohibits contact with a menstruating woman. In Hebrew, she is termed a '*niddah*,' a word meaning 'separated' or 'excluded.'" (Eisenberg, 557ff.) The term niddah has also been defined as meaning "ceremonial impurity, especially of menstruation," "impure thing," "excretion, abhorrent thing," "impurity, menstruation," "abomination," "filth, menstrual uncleanness," "something unclean, or filthy," etc. (De Troyer, 15.)

Men have authority over women because God has
made the one superior to the other, and because
they spend their wealth to maintain them. Good
women are obedient.[1]

In his infinite compassion, God/Allah has made
woman a simply horrible creature! Of course, the
worst punishments are those for individuals, male *and*

female, who simply refuse to
believe in these concepts, mere
unbelief serving as the most
egregious transgression of all.

In Buddhism too has reigned
a sexist attitude in many places,
with the belief, for example, that a
woman can only attain to
Buddhahood if she reincarnates
first as a man. As stated by Dr.
Serinity Young, a professor at Columbia University:

Texts like the *Pure Land, Astasaharikaprajnaparamita,
Lotus sutras*, and several others, insist one must
become a man before achieving enlightenment
because one of the marks of an enlightened being is
a sheathed penis, one of the thirty-two marks of the
historical Buddha. Even with an unusual penis, the
male remains the normative human, and when a
woman becomes a man she achieves higher
status.[2]

Scholarly debates abound on the depth and nature
of sexism and misogyny in various Buddhist sects over
the centuries since the alleged time of "the historical
Buddha."[3] The sexism in Japanese Buddhism is
described by Dr. DeMeo:

Puritanism...spread into Japan during the 800s
through the agency of Confucian and Buddhist
scholars. They preached chastity for women,
concubines for men, and placed taboos on

---

[1] Dawood (1990), 64.
[2] Young, 197.
[3] See, e.g., Gross and Gutschow.

remarriage of widows or female divorcees.... Women were seen as the root of all evil, and vaginal blood taboos and cleaning rituals appeared. Vaginal blood was feared as a poison by the common man, and Buddhist priests were appointed to deflower virgin brides on their wedding night....[1]

In some formal Buddhist gatherings to this day, the nuns—with heads shaved—are segregated from the monks and made to sit in the back. We also find plenty of stories concerning sexual abuse of women within Tibetan (Tantric) Buddhism, particularly from those who serve as *songyums* or *dakinis*, special words to describe individuals who often end up as little more than sex slaves.[2]

## Burning Women is Not Sacred

Within fundamentalist Hinduism as well over the centuries, women often have been treated badly, exemplified by the burning alive of women called *sati* or *suttee*. In a chapter entitled, "Suttee and the Hindu Scriptures," Oxford lecturer Dr. Edward John Thompson (1886-1946) relates:

The rite by which a Hindu widow became *sati*, "faithful," had two forms: *sahamarana*, "dying in company with," and *anumarana*, "dying in accordance with."...

In the *Mahabharata*, one of the two widows of Pandu is, after a lengthy argument between her and her co-wife as to which is entitled to the privilege, allowed as a high honour to share her husband's pyre. Four

---

[1] DeMeo, 357.
[2] See June Campbell, Vallely. See also Evinger's *Clergy Sexual Abuse: Annotated Bibliography of Conceptual and Practical Resources.*

of Krishna's wives and four of Vasudeva's burned on their lord's death...[1]

Here we see that not only did the exalted Indian god Krishna have multiple wives—16,000 by some accounts![2]—but also at least four were incinerated upon his demise. The parts in the Mahabharata concerning sati may be later interpolations included to give authority and antiquity to this practice. Dr. Thompson further relates that the Indian sacred text the *Ramayana* does not discuss sati, while the *Tantras* proscribe it.[3] Concerning the frequency of sati, Dr. John Stratton Hawley, a professor of Religion at Columbia University Hawley states, "Modern research confirms what traditional brahmanical treatises imply—that sati has always been very much the exception rather than the rule in Hindu life."[4]

Over the centuries, sati was banned in several places in India but was not easily put down, even though it was criminalized in 1829 by the British, who actively suppressed sati during the 19th and 20th centuries. Regarding the state of sati in India over the past several decades, Dr. Hawley remarks:

After India became an independent nation in 1947, occasional stories appeared in the newspapers about a sati in some remote village in Madhya Pradesh or Rajasthan. Through the 1970s and 1980s, however, either incidents of sati increased or greater scrutiny was brought to bear on the issue, primarily by women's organizations....[5]

---

[1] Thompson, 15-18.
[2] Bryant, *KBLG*, 265, 266.
[3] Thompson, 19.
[4] Hawley, 3.
[5] Hawley, 47.

A sati was committed most notoriously in 1987 involving a woman named Roop Kanwar, who became a figure around whom Indian women rallied to make the practice intolerable to enlightened Indian society.[1] In response to their protests arose a counter-protest, as Hawley further reports:

> In 1987, a Sati Dharma Raksha Samiti ("Committee for the Defense of the Religion of Sati") sent 70,000 pro-sati demonstrators into the streets of Jaipur shouting for the same cause [to defend the Hindu right to sati].[2]

Hawley also relates:

> New temples to the goddess Sati have been constructed in many of India's great cities. This same goddess, depicted as a multi-armed woman sitting on a bed of flames, comprises the logo for an importer of basmati rice with branches all over the United States. The chunari celebration following a sati that occurred in 1987 at Deorala, some 50 miles from Jaipur in the state of Rajasthan, drew 200,000 to 300,000 people.[3]

Despite the outcry, sati obviously continues to receive surprising support, and widow burning is still practiced on occasion in isolated areas "mostly...in parts of northern and central India," occurring as recently as 2002 and 2006, for example.[4]

Regarding cruel and anti-female traditions in India, DeMeo relates that the Indo-Aryans "brought with them the seeds of Hinduism, the caste system, infant cranial deformation, a general view of the woman as inferior, vaginal blood taboos, and the practice of ritual widow murder (*suttee* or *sati* which in Sanskrit means "chaste woman") or mother-murder."[5] In describing the well-known "voluptuous female statues" of India,

---

[1] Hawley, 6.
[2] Hawley, 4.
[3] Hawley, 4.
[4] "India wife dies on husband's pyre,"
news.bbc.co.uk/2/hi/south_asia/5273336.stm
[5] DeMeo, 289.

DeMeo further states that they are "abundant within temples and palaces of [patriarchal] Hindu India, made to please dominant males (kings, priests, etc.) to whom women were subordinated or enslaved."[1] Unfortunately, because of such biases and societal pressures rooted in antiquity, India today is notorious for gender-selective abortions targeting female fetuses.[2]

## Genital Mutilation is Not Holy

In addition to the psycho-spiritual abuse, around the globe women are used as beasts of burden,  babymaking machines and readily available sex-toys, and this attitude and treatment are constantly justified by men and women alike as somehow both necessary and righteous. Worldwide over 130 million women[3]—mostly Muslim[4]—have been hideously mutilated and disfigured at the hands of deranged fanatics who apparently believe that their Creator screwed up when he endowed women with genitals, which must be violently removed in "rituals" that often include the use of rusty knives or pieces of metal, or broken glass. The women, girls and female infants who undergo these rituals are generally not anesthetized but are often held down by other women, who

---

[1] DeMeo, 303.

[2] See, e.g., Patel.

[3] "Female Genital Cutting," www.womenshealth.gov/faq/female-genital-cutting.cfm.

[4] Although it is not sanctioned in the Koran, millions of people in Egypt and Somalia, for example, believe female genital mutilation to be an *Islamic* practice ordained by Allah through Mohammed. As stated by the Muslim Women's League: "Those who advocate for FGM from an Islamic perspective commonly quote the following hadith to argue that it is required as part of the Sunnah or Tradition of the Prophet:

*"Um Atiyyat al-Ansariyyah said: A woman used to perform circumcision in Medina. The Prophet (pbuh) said to her: Do not cut too severely as that is better for a woman and more desirable for a husband."*

evidently sheepishly and shamelessly go along with the dictates of men. These women and girls also frequently receive no post-mutilation care, and they sometimes bleed to death, with cascades of blood showering their feet.

### Ankles are a Sexual Turn-on?!

In these same and other parts of the world, women are beaten, imprisoned, tortured, burned and sometimes killed for exposing their faces, hair, ankles or wrists, not to mention any other part of their bodies. Women are viewed as delicious temptresses who, unless subdued, would quickly destroy a man's morality. The weakness of the man is never blamed. He just can't help himself if he sees a beautiful, "seductive" woman exposed; he must have her or go mad. Thus, instead of learning to control their animalistic urges, these men put the blame on the women, who are then subjected to their full fury. Women are also worked to the bone and must keep reproducing or lose whatever little status they continue to hold. Moreover, the constant covering up of their skin, thus depriving it of health-bestowing sunlight, leads to horrible bone problems such as osteoporosis, osteomalacia, etc. Indeed, this deficiency state is happening to Muslim women, especially in Iran, Saudi Arabia and Taliban-dominated parts of Pakistan and Afghanistan, where they are also starving, because they are prevented from working.[1]

According to these various religious systems, actions have little to do with a person's worth, but gender certainly does; hence, "God" is utterly sexist. Is it any wonder, then, why sexism and misogyny refuse to fade into oblivion? It is dictated from the "Creator"

---

[1] Green, "Afghan Women Brutalized by the Taliban."

on down. In fact, sexism is to be practiced as "God's will!"

## There is Nothing Religious About Depravity

Too many people are afraid to condemn heinous and egregious behavior, claiming to be "tolerant" and "respectful" of someone else's religion. This attitude shows how deeply the abuse has penetrated the human psyche. Millennia have elapsed during which these "memes" or units of mental programming have been passed down from generation to generation—so insidious is the notion that abusing women is somehow justifiable! The fact that this atrocious behavior and attitude towards women are justified by religion is one of the greatest hypocrisies of the human species.

Indeed, this situation ranks as a powerful slap in the face of the "Creator"—i.e., the divine creative life principle—which has endowed in human beings infinite abilities and creative genius well beyond the simple urges of bonding and reproducing. If one were truly religious, one would feel compelled to utilize one's "God-given" talents to the fullest, utterly appreciating them and being grateful for them. But instead, they are suppressed and denied to the point of nonexistence. In truth, if one were seriously concerned with living the divine life, in accordance to righteous principles, one would be thoroughly obliged to use any extraordinary skills and talents for the good of humanity and the betterment of all life upon this small planet, regardless of one's gender. Forcing people into soul-deadening roles based on their gender constitutes the antithesis of a godly or righteous experience: Such sexism destroying divine creativity is in effect *anti-God.* Using one's *God*-given intelligence, creativity and talents to their utmost would represent the true fulfillment of the will of any good deity, if one existed. Unfortunately, in many places women are neither encouraged nor allowed to develop any such sublime and godly gifts.

This abusive behavior towards women flies in the face of the real religious or spiritual experience. Again, the oppression and denigration of women are anti-God and unspiritual, and create such an enormous amount of suffering and horror as cannot be measured. No intelligent, thinking person could possibly go along with it, yet tens and hundreds of millions of people do, every day, day in and day out. A truly spiritual person will strive to end this abhorrent mistreatment, rather than to perpetuate it. The perpetuation of suffering is not a religious experience by any stretch of imagination. It is an abomination.

### "God" is Not a Man—Get It?!![1]

Much of this atrocity comes from the sexist notion that "God"—the Divine—is exclusively male, that there simply is no female aspect in creation. Obviously, to enlightened people, this notion is wrong—an erroneous idea born of men's desire to control and lord over

women. Creation is composed of both male and female, in equal proportions, and until that balance is established, there will never be harmony and an end to misery on earth. A truly spiritual individual is neither male nor female, black nor white. As even the Bible says:

> "There is neither Jew nor Greek, there is neither slave nor free, there is neither male nor female; for you are all one in Christ Jesus." (Gal 3:28)

"Christ Jesus" does not necessarily refer to a Jewish man who allegedly lived 2,000 years ago, as the phrase means in Greek "the Anointed One by whom Yahweh Saves." This phrase could refer to a mechanism by which one becomes enlightened. In the end, the "Christed" or enlightened individual is

---

[1] Disclaimer: This rant is not "anti-male." In mistreating women, the world's men are missing out on a great deal of beauty, joy and love.

nothing and everything, including both genders and no gender. Let us be unified yet recognize and welcome the variety in the cosmos!

# A Question of Free Will

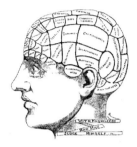

"Submit yourselves therefore to God. Resist the devil and he will flee from you."

James 4:7

"Lord, make us submissive to You; make of our descendants a nation that will submit to You..."[1]

Koran 2:127

"...Job's question remains a valid one: why do evil things happen to good people? One answer is free will."

Dr. Dinesh D'Souza, *What's So Great About Christianity* (277)

"If the origin of evil is free will, and God is the origin of free will, isn't God then the origin of evil?"

Dr. Peter Kreeft, *Fundamentals of Christian Apologetics* (56)

In the realm of religious debate, we frequently come upon the subject of free will. Whenever something bad occurs, sensible people ask the question, "Where is God when things like this happen?" Where is the precious Almighty when good people are hideously killed, crushed to death in cars, slammed to the ground in airplanes, or tortured and murdered by psychopaths? The main answer the

---

[1] Dawood (1990), 22.

theologians and apologists can come up with is that God gave us "free will."

What a nice idea! We have FREE WILL. These are words to soothe the masses and explain away the atrocities that could not happen in a world which was truly under the care of an omniscient and omnipotent deity. Yet, under this totalitarian system of government proposed by God-cheerleaders, free will is *not* allowed, because we *must* believe in him or suffer all eternity in the fires of hell! If we "free will" humans do not slavishly follow God's commandments or "believe unto" him, his son, his prophet or some other such notion, we will be severely punished. So much for free will.

Now, this contention constitutes schizophrenia, plain and simple. Certain individuals are running about squawking out of both sides of their mouths, "We have free will" and "We have to go to church/temple/mosque/synagogue, or God will be mad at us." The God-fearers' motto is, "Have free will, but be sure to march off mindlessly to church, temple or mosque because someone else has told you to!" Such folks unfortunately resemble addled robots, not free-will beings. To claim that God rules everything and we must submit to his will, yet we have our own free will, represents broken-brained thinking. How do we reconcile these irreconcilable concepts? By what bizarre quirk of our minds can we do such an illogical thing? We can't have it both ways.

### Obey Your Masters!

Indeed, while they may be saying "free will," they are fanatically following a book purportedly written by God that says: "Let every person be subject to the governing authorities. For there is no authority except from God, and those that exist have been instituted by God." (Romans 13:17) Does this scripture sound even remotely that God gave anybody "free will?" How about this exhortation at 1 Pet 2:13-18:

Be subject for the Lord's sake to every human institution, whether it be to the emperor as supreme, or to governors as sent by him to punish those who do wrong and to praise those who do right. For it is **God's will** that by doing right you should put to silence the ignorance of foolish men. Live as free men, yet without using your freedom as a pretext of evil; but live as servants of God. Honor all men. Love the brotherhood. Fear God. Honor the emperor.

Servants, be submissive to your masters with all respect, not only to the kind and gentle but also to the overbearing. (Emphasis added.)

Other authoritarian biblical messages include:

Let all who are under the yoke of slavery regard their masters as worthy of all honor, so that the name of God and the teaching may not be defamed. (1 Tim 6:1)

Bid slaves to be submissive to their masters and give satisfaction in every respect... (Tit 2:9)

Obey your leaders and submit to them; for they are keeping watch over your souls. (Heb 13-17)

The apostle Paul is relentless in his anti-free-will dictates:

Wives, be subject to your husbands, as is fitting in the Lord.... Children, obey your parents in everything, for this pleases the Lord.... Slaves, obey in everything those who are your earthly masters... (Col 3:18-22)

Wives, be subject to your husbands, as to the Lord. For the husband is the head of the wife as Christ is the head of the church, his body, and is himself its Savior. As the church is subject to Christ, so let wives also be subject in everything to their husbands. (Eph 5:22-24)

At 1 Tim 2:11-15, the apostle exhorts:

Let a woman learn in silence with all submissiveness.
I permit no woman to teach or to have authority over
men; she is to keep silent. For Adam was formed
first, then Eve; and Adam was not deceived, but the
woman was deceived and became a transgressor. Yet
woman will be saved through bearing children, if she
continues in faith and love and holiness, with
modesty.

Does any of this twaddle resemble free will? Slaves
obeying masters and women being forced to be
submissive, quiet and bear children to redeem their
supposed transgressions? Of course, the Adam-Eve
fable is just another sexist device propagated by men,
as is the rest of this anti-woman gibberish.

 How about God making his
stiff-necked people eat their
offspring because they did not love
and fear him? (Deut 28:53, et seq.)
Or Abraham being commanded to
murder his son? (Gen 22) Like the
New Testament, the OT is glutted
with authoritarian demands on the
part of God. Does such theocracy
truly represent free will?

Of course, there are words interspersed here and
there to soften such messages, such as "live as free
men," but these are quickly followed by anti-free-will
dictates such as "live as servants of God.... Fear God.
Honor the emperor." It is obvious that vested interests
such as priests and emperors are at work here. And it
is equally evident that "free will" in religion is not free
will at all. It's all a grand mind-game, to be polite.

## Slaves of Allah

Moreover, the very word "Islam" means submission, and the Koran too is full of exhortations that a true believer must essentially be a *slave* to Allah. The authoritarian nature of Islam is thus expressed in a number of koranic verses or *suras/ surahs*:

> The only true faith in God's sight is Islam.[1] (Koran 3:19)

> He that chooses a religion over Islam, it will not be accepted from him and in the world to come he will be one of the lost.[2] (Koran 3:86)

> It is not for true believers men or women to take their choice in the affairs if God and His apostle decree otherwise. He that disobeys God and His apostle strays far indeed.[3] (Koran 33:36)

> Men have authority over women because God has made the one superior to the other, and because they spend their wealth to maintain them. Good women are obedient.[4] (Koran 4:34)

Obviously, there is little room for free will within Islam. In fact, quite the opposite, as unless we wish to be condemned to hell in the afterlife or tortured and murdered in this life, we must submit ourselves to Islam:

> God's curse be upon the infidels! Evil is that for which they have bartered away their souls. To deny God's own revelation, grudging that He should reveal His bounty to whom He chooses from among His servants! They have incurred God's most inexorable

---

[1] Dawood (1990), 44.
[2] Dawood (1990), 50.
[3] Dawood (1990), 296.
[4] Dawood (1990), 64.

wrath. An ignominious punishment awaits the unbelievers.[1] (Koran 2:92-6)

Concerning a man's right to marry a woman, the Koran (4:24) remarks, "Also [forbidden to you are] married women, except those whom you own as slaves."[2] Thus, we discover that it is allowable in Islam to own women as slaves—what happened to *their* free will? Indeed, in some parts of the Koran, it seems taken for granted that Muslims will own slaves, such as at 24:58: "Believers, let your slaves and those who are under age ask your leave on three occasions when they come to see you..."[3] Where is *their* free will? In reality, again, the very word "Islam" means "submission," so it hardly represents anything resembling free will, and, again, its followers frequently refer to themselves as "slaves of Allah." No self-respecting individual would be pleased by such a title, and this need for Allah to enslave humanity like a bunch of BORG does not make him appear to be a god of any sort but, rather, a vicious tyrant. This very notion would represent an *insult* to any truly good and merciful God.

### Is God Negligent?

In addition, why do religionists constantly apologize for God, who, according to them, is not participating at all in creation, unless it is convenient to their arguments that he exists? When a plane crashes, the survivors thank "the Lord" for allowing them to live. What about those who died? Did the

[1] Dawood (1990), 18.
[2] Dawood (2006), 81.
[3] Dawood (2006), 356.

Lord let them die? And where was the Lord when the plane was hurtling out of the sky, terrifying its passengers to the point of psychosis? According to believers, God is not involved in that aspect of the tragedy, only in the saving of certain people, with whom he is apparently well pleased. Did the others deserve to die? The typical excuse offered up when confronted with this flaw in thinking goes something like this: "The Lord has called them home, for reasons only he can understand." In other words, the slippery canard: "God works in mysterious ways." Now, this is a sadistic god, who, although omniscient and therefore able to see what is going to happen ahead of time, and omnipotent and therefore able to prevent it, allows the shite to hit the fan again and again, never lifting a finger. Hey, how about letting us in on the plan? Don't we "free will" beings deserve to be treated with some respect?

And what about the absurd thinking behind the notion of a Jewish fellow dying on a cross thousands of years ago somehow absolving us of our sins today? What do he and his death have to do with us? Somehow blind belief can reconcile these illogical concepts as well. What does this purported redemption and salvation through belief truly mean? Does this scenario mean that so long as we believe in Jesus or Allah, we can do whatever we wish, because we cannot sin? Are we free to rape, pillage and murder, so long as we are "good" Christians, Jews or Muslims? Why don't we all just do that then, because we will automatically

be absolved of such heinous behavior if we just "confess the Lord Jesus Christ with our mouths and hearts" or some other such notion?

Indeed, vast armies of "good Christians" and "pious Muslims" have done just that, freely and with clear conscience marauding and slaughtering all who got in their path, while holding up the banner of Jesus, Yahweh or Allah. Do Christians think Christ would be pleased by such behavior? If so, why is anyone following him, who sheepishly "turned his cheek" yet violently overturned the moneychangers' tables? If he would not be pleased, why has not his Omnipotence put his foot down and made an appearance, setting his followers straight? The common excuse is that he gave us free will! Free will to murder and pillage as we wish—what a great gift!

If we have free will, then *we are also free not to believe in the male Jewish-Arab God/Allah or Jesus in the first place*, without risking eternal hellfire or any other sadistic punishment by the megalomaniacal and tyrannical Almighty. We can be free not to believe in some hallowed god person separate and apart from a wretched creation but, rather, to perceive the entire cosmos as divine. Out of our free will, we can choose not to harm other sentient beings (and even humans), regardless of what religious leaders beckon us to do. We can choose to reject being part of a herd of panicky sheep who turn into wolves when it benefits them. Out of free will, we can be "free agents" who do not belong to religious cults of any sort. Indeed, without "God's plan," we can be free to create our own vision, one of a world not divided by spurious creeds based in myth and used to justify racism and sexism. With our boundless free will, we can create a utopia of unified humanity. Free of our god-addiction, we can be free to just be.

### "Let my freethinkers go!"

freethought:

"the liberty to question and doubt unscientific and uncritical beliefs, especially as concerns religion"

# Celebration of Life

"Life must celebrate life each day, every day, however the day may begin, or whatever the day may bring, however we might do the celebration. The celebration of life must never stop as long as mankind is on this earth, and we each have breath. To celebrate is to emphasize the positive and not the negative."

Cecil Mark Inman, *A Celebration of Life* (222)

What is the purpose in life? Is it simply to follow rules and rote that turn people into robots and drones? It is clear that human beings, free from stifling and enslaving ideologies, can become great, exalted and divine. While it is crucial and good to engage in the breaking down of divisive and dangerous beliefs that make human beings less glorious than they truly are, it is also necessary to identify that glory, such that we may all strive to attain to it. The human experience is largely one of extremes, and we have seen how negative extremes have manifested themselves in the human species and in the natural world around them. We have attempted to destroy these detrimental divisions. Now is the time to reveal the beauty and vivacity of the butterfly that emerges when the dead and desiccated cocoon is removed.

## When are Human Beings at Their Best?

When human beings have fully blossomed, when they've reached a certain level of soul maturity that is balanced, neither too aggressive nor too ineffectual, they are a wonder to behold, bursting with life and love. These divine beings have a tremendous sense of humor, knowing well that there is no reason to take this long, strange trip seriously. This wondrous state of being requires not extraordinary intelligence but wisdom, which can be found even within a tiny seed. The intelligence the enlightened condition does require is that which compels all living creatures to be truly alive. This natural state is in fact the same in which animals live; it is not difficult to attain. Yet, because of ego encrustation, many people cannot regain this experience, which is that of childhood.

People at their best maintain the awe and wonder of a child while developing the responsibility and integrity of true adulthood. They are sensitive and empathetic, sharing in the pain of others and providing remedy. Yet, they are not emotional basketcases who become too debilitated by tragedy for their own good and that of others. Unfortunately, such an experience may be necessary for a soul to mature, but there comes a time when one has had enough misfortune and demands change for one's own life, those of loved ones and of all life in general. The metamorphosis into a true human being can be propelled by the painful experiences. At the point of blooming, one has truly decided that pain is to be avoided and that one's actions will be designed to provoke the most amount of happiness and bliss.

The ability to change instantly a bad situation into a good one is not so easily gained; yet, it is at times like these, when people pull together and bring off masterful miracles, that human beings really shine. For, during these moments of catastrophe, whether it be an earthquake, other act of nature or human tragedy, division and prejudice are cast aside, and glorious heroes are created. So, the blossoming individual rates as a hero or heroine. But this statement need not be construed as hero worship or as an encouragement for people to be overly heroic such that they endanger themselves or others; it simply reflects that when these moments happen, they reveal the best of the human being. A heroic action is not the only time that the best is revealed, obviously. And, obviously, we'd prefer to avoid catastrophes in the first place. As they say, it is unfortunate it takes tragedy to bring out the best in people.

When human beings take it on their own initiative to right a wrong or better a situation, regardless of any ideology, they are at their luscious best. When they are selfless enough to step in where needed and responsible enough to be concerned about others and their environment. When they have the class to be gracious and forgiving—this quality is when humans reach perfection.

## Humans Can Be Radiant and Superb

Human beings are also at their best when they are around animals and babies, which can be perfectly enjoyable in a perfect world. Children are frequently simply amazing beings who express endless joy and love. It is true that although they are not very cognizant, babies are teachers, in that they provide examples of various aspects of our true nature. And this natural, innocent state of babyhood is one reason why people have children: To experience vicariously their awe  and bliss, which represent divine qualities. Of course, not all children are fortunate enough to have this rapturous life. But humans at their best strive to provide all others, including animals, with this ultimate life experience of being surrounded by love and wonderment. Animals, of course, frequently bring out the best in humans, in many different situations. Pets no doubt give many people much thrill at being alive. Like babies, some animals are truly adorable and can get a smile out of the worst grouch. And baby animals could melt an iceberg.

People are also at their best when they participate in group activities that are pure and raw, not repeating rote as in church, temple, synagogue or mosque, but singing songs of many types, cheering on others, going on nature walks or dancing in ecstasy.

Humans are also wonderful when they are creative.

When creating, humans are about as divine as they can become, since creativity is the realm of the creator. Creativity *is* the creator. Creativity is art, and vice versa. The greatest works of art move us profoundly, whether they be paintings, photos, films or literature. But an equation that solves the world's energy needs or a medical technique that allows for normal life are also great works of art. An environmentally friendly community is art. Art includes beautiful performances that stir us to laughter and tears, such as singing, dancing or figure skating. Even a great athletic competition can be art. As would be a less popular battle of the wits. And, in a world where overpopulation is not a problem, creating another life is a wondrous work of art. "Art" can basically be defined as the striving for excellence in any field, subject or interest. This striving for excellence, however, does not represent the neurotic quest for perfection in which one self-flagellates or bludgeons others for perceived small mistakes. This quest for excellence is a celebration along the way; it is enjoyable in itself. The artist knows there will always be flaws but may attempt to reduce them, purely for the pleasure of doing so, of improving, but not out of some frenzied and desperate sense.

When creating art of any sort, humans are sublime and celestial. They represent the ideal of the universe, the pinnacle of creation itself. They are angels and gods. And this sublimity is one reason human beings are cherished, and why the human incarnation, as bad as it can get, is so desirable.

Another reason the human experience is so alluring is because of love and sex, pure and simple. It would not be an overstatement that every living creature enjoys feeling ecstasy, that blissful rush which dissolves the boundaries of existence. Thus, the delectable sensation attracts randy souls from around the cosmos. Many are vying for time on this plane, despite its serious pitfalls, because the return to the Void from here is a helluva ride! Or a heaven of a ride, as the case may be. But, this thrill for life can be experienced through the body, by a variety of methods from art to sports to meditation. Besides the physical ecstasy, however, there is spiritual euphoria, which serves to reconnect a soul with its source, and here again is when humans become divine. This "cosmic orgasm" reveals the illusion of creation and the oneness of all. It also brings the understanding that while souls may be encased within separate identities, they are all part of the purity and beauty of the whole. And the true love produced between human beings sets the cosmos itself on fire. It lights up the whole universe. This state of evolution is when humans at are their best.

Humans are also at their ultimate best when they are not constantly focused on being with people but can walk through the woods, climb a hill or lie in a meadow, where the aroma of flowers grabs their attention and makes them look closer at their surroundings. People are fully alive when

they are in nature, when their feet are massaged by grass or sand, when they are sitting silently against a tree, listening to the music of the birds and the wind. Humans are at their finest when they are lying under a starry sky projecting themselves into the vast and miraculous unknown. This communion with nature is one with the entire cosmos. It is, indeed, a celebration of life.

# A Truly Sacred Scripture

*Scripture:*

*1. a. A sacred writing or book.*
 *b. A passage from such a writing or book.*
*2. The sacred writings of the Bible. Often used in the plural. Also called Holy Scriptures.*
*3. A statement regarded as authoritative.*[1]

What is a sacred or holy scripture? Hundreds of millions of people around the world hold sacred the Bible, the Koran, the Lotus Sutra, the Vedas, Puranas and other texts considered to be "divinely inspired" in some way or another. Countless people claim that there is a single god somewhere "out there" who directly inspired these various texts, which are therefore infallible, since this god "himself" is infallible. Others see these writings as manmade and containing errors, although they may also possess much divinely inspired wisdom. Still others consider these so-called scriptures to be entirely contrived by human beings and a reflection of *human* understanding, rather than divine inspiration.

What is the truth? Is a book that contains endless stories of warfare and slaughter against infidels or unbelieving nations and individuals really "holy writ?" One which dictates that there are "chosen people" who are superior to others, who may thus be unreservedly dominated and exploited? Or that human beings are

---

[1] *American Heritage Dictionary*, 1103.

revolting "sinners" who can only achieve grace by believing in a "Son of God" who was hideously tortured and murdered "for our sins?" Or that infidels are inferior subhumans who can be brutalized, terrorized and enslaved in this life, while viciously punished in the afterlife? Is this sort of "scripture" truly the most appropriate and intelligent writing *the* God of the cosmos could come up with?

Let us briefly examine some of what these "holy scriptures" say:

> For you are a people holy to the LORD your God; the LORD your God has chosen you to be a people for his own possession, out of all the peoples that are on the face of the earth. (Deuteronomy 7:6)

> You shall suck the milk of nations, you shall suck the breast of kings; and you shall know that I, the LORD, am your Savior and your Redeemer, the Mighty One of Jacob. (Isaiah 60:16)

> Do not think that I have come to bring peace on earth; I have not come to bring peace, but a sword. For I have come to set a man against his father, and a daughter against her mother, and a daughter-in-law against her mother-in-law; and a man's foes will be those of his own household. He who loves father or mother more than me is not worthy. (Matthew 10:34-37)

> If any one comes to me and does not hate his own father and mother and wife and children and brothers and sisters, yes, and even his own life, he cannot be my disciple. (Luke 14:26)

> For nation will rise up against nation, and kingdom against kingdom, and there will be famines and earthquakes in various places: all this is but the beginning of the sufferings. (Matthew 24:7-8)

This Book is not to be doubted.... As for the unbelievers, it is the same whether or not you forewarn them; they will not have faith. God has set a seal upon their hearts and ears; their sight is dimmed and grievous punishment awaits them.[1] (Koran 2:2-6)

God's curse be upon the infidels! Evil is that for which they have bartered away their souls. To deny God's own revelation, grudging that He should reveal His bounty to whom He chooses from among His servants! They have incurred God's most inexorable wrath. An ignominious punishment awaits the unbelievers.[2] (Koran 2:92-6)

Phew! That's a whole lotta spewing. Now, of course, this collection represents only a fraction of the calumny and vitriol contained in those "holy texts." But, naturally, there is some "good" stuff to balance it...slightly. Yet, again, is this type of sentiment—which permeates not only the so-called scriptures but also the ideologies themselves, oozing out of believers like some supercilious and smug sludge, heartlessly hurled at all who do not believe likewise—really the best and holiest concept in the cosmos, such that it merits the distinction of being deemed "divinely inspired" and representing the "inerrant Word of God?"

Or could there be something much more enlightened that deserves to be held up in a higher sacrosanct position?

We the people of the United States, in order to form a more perfect union, establish justice, insure domestic tranquility, provide for the common defense, promote the general welfare, and secure the blessings of liberty to ourselves and our posterity, do ordain and establish this Constitution for the United States of America.

---

[1] Dawood (1990), 11.
[2] Dawood (1990), 18.

The American Constitution may well be the "holiest of holies." It is not "inerrant," nor does it address religion specifically, except for this particularly pithy amendment that is not only wholly relevant but also *holy* in its implications for securing liberty from religious imposition of all kinds:

> Congress shall make no law respecting an establishment of religion, or prohibiting the free exercise thereof; or abridging the freedom of speech, or of the press; or the right of the people peaceably to assemble, and to petition the government for a redress of grievances.

These remarks do not suggest that the constitutions of other nations are necessarily inferior or that the U.S. is flawless, but at least in this well-considered and well-written *scripture*—as defined by the third definition: "A statement regarded as authoritative"—there is a chance for humanity to be truly free and to reach its highest potential.

If we were to fling open the doors of nations around the world and allow free movement in either direction, which way would most of the traffic flow? Would most people up and run towards "Oppressivestan," under the dominion of so-called holy law, or towards "Libertyland," governed by such a constitution? Think about it.

# Epilogue

THE CULPEPER MINUTE MEN

LIBERTY OR DEATH

DONT TREAD ON ME

"The condition upon which God hath given liberty to man is eternal vigilance..."[1]

> John Philpot Curran, *Speeches of John Philpot Curran* (5)

"I claim free speech as my religion. Yes, I'll have a slice of that pie too, thank you, along with all the attendant rights and privileges, of course. Because I can assure you that I venerate free speech as highly as anybody on this planet venerates their god or their scripture or their prophet, and any attempt to suppress free speech is deeply insulting and grossly offensive to me on a personal level. I feel violated to the very core of my being, which seriously hurts my feelings. Whenever I hear free speech being compromised or restricted—or even heavily criticized—I take that as a grave personal affront and as a grotesquely insensitive attack on my most cherished values: Freedom of thought, freedom of speech, freedom of identity—this is my holy trinity. Each one an intrinsic aspect of my god. Freedom, the holiest of holies. Yes, it bloody well is. It is absolutely sacred and inviolable beyond any negotiation or compromise now and forever. Amen."

> Pat Condell, "Free Speech is Sacred"

Like the essays "Born in Sin?" and "Celebration of Life," the treatise, "A Truly Sacred Scripture" was not originally part of *The Gospel According to Acharya S.*

---

[1] Chapman, 130.

After I initially posted the Gospel online at
TruthBeKnown.com, a number of people requested
that I create an essay describing what I felt was the
result of human endeavors, a positive image of the
self-realized human being; hence, I wrote "Celebration
of Life" sometime toward the end of the 1990s. I
published "A Truly Sacred Scripture" on March 29,
2006, as part of my blog TBKNews.blogspot.com,
which was new at the time.

At this point in history, I feel it is crucial that all
peoples interested in freedom stand up for the
extraordinary values encased within the U.S.
Constitution. Thus, I deemed it imperative to include
"A Truly Sacred Scripture" in this book, which is
intended to impart a sense of sacredness to our
experience as free human beings on planet Earth.
Without the U.S. Constitution—and unfortunately
there simply is no other governing system quite like
it—true human civilization would be nearly impossible
to attain. At this critical time, we are battling the worst
onslaught against human rights ever on a global basis.
Like the rest of this Gospel, I would like to see
hundreds of millions of people take "A Truly Sacred
Scripture" to heart and insist that the U.S.
Constitution not only be protected from this offensive
against our freedoms but also that its human-
respecting and life-affirming philosophy be spread
around the world, to every land and culture where
people cherish liberty.

This exhortation does not serve as a call for
American imperialism, in the sense that the U.S.
Constitution should be compelled whole cloth upon
other nations or upon a global government. Rather, we
are interested in seeing the major *principles* of
individual human and civil rights that the Constitution
and its Amendments embody—such as liberty and
justice for all—be applied on a worldwide basis. This
"sacred scripture" may be and has been used in
creating new constitutions in other lands that factor in
the ethnic and other needs of the people(s) whom it is

designed to protect. It is the overarching wisdom concerning human integrity and individual potential behind the Constitution that needs to be extended globally.

Our forefathers in many parts of the world fought too hard for the liberties we enjoy now for us to let them go so easily. As American Founding Father and President Thomas Jefferson (1743-1826) purportedly remarked, "The price for freedom is eternal vigilance."[1] If we do not defend the principles behind the U.S. Constitution—no matter what land we live in—we *will* be enslaved by one of the most fascistic ideologies ever devised by mankind. I refer, of course, to so-called holy law, which is not "holy" but was concocted to exploit the weak and prey upon the poor and downtrodden, to enslave human beings and commit brutal acts upon them at every turn.

A Constitution of this sort should be the law of the land worldwide. Few of the alternative forms of governance contain all the liberties, freedoms and human rights afforded to every single human being regardless of race, ethnicity, religion, gender or age as can be found in the U.S. Constitution. Indeed, the alternatives in other nations often border on slavery, and many people of those countries cry out for help. We will be less human ourselves if we do not attempt to assist them.

In this regard, please take the Constitutional values to heart and make sure that you speak out against the would-be enslavers of mankind, regardless of their nationality, ethnicity, race, religion or political leanings. And be certain to use these rights to protect your own freedoms, as elucidated in this gospel, if indeed you find these concepts worthy of defending as sacred truths.

---

[1] This saying is not found in any of Jefferson's writings or recorded speeches. The earliest rendition of this quote may be from a speech by Irish lawyer John Philpot Curran (1750-1817), published in 1805.

# Bibliography

"Ardhanarishvara in Art and Philosophy,"
www.exoticindiaart.com/article/ardhanarishvara/

"The Dionysian Mysteries," www.lost-history.com/mysteries5.php

"Edward King, Viscount Kingsborough,"
en.wikipedia.org/wiki/Lord_Kingsborough

"Fall of Man," en.wikipedia.org/wiki/Fall_of_Man

"Female Genital Cutting,"
www.womenshealth.gov/faq/female-genital-cutting.cfm

"India wife dies on husband's pyre,"
news.bbc.co.uk/2/hi/south_asia/5273336.stm

"Priene Inscription,"
www.artsci.wustl.edu/~fkflinn/Priene Inscription.html

Abramovitch, Ilana and Galvin, Sean, *Jews of Brooklyn*, Brandeis University Press, 2001.

Acharya S, *The Christ Conspiracy: The Greatest Story Ever Sold*, AUP, IL, 1999.
—*Suns of God: Krishna, Buddha and Christ Unveiled*, AUP, IL, 2004.

Akerley, Ben Edward, *The X-Rated Bible*, Feral House, Los Angeles, 1999.

Allen, James P., *Middle Egyptian: An Introduction to the Language and Culture of Hieroglyphs*, Cambridge University Press, 2000.

*The American College Dictionary*, Random House, 1970.

*The American Heritage Dictionary*, Houghton Mifflin, NY, 1982.

Anthony, David W., *The Horse, the Wheel and Language*, Princeton University Press, 2007.

Barker, Dan, *Losing Faith in Faith*, FFRF, Inc., 2006.

*The Bible*, Revised Standard Version, Williams Collins & Sons, NY/Glasgow/Toronto, 1946, 1952.

Bryant, Edwin F., ed., *Krishna: The Beautiful Legend of God (Srimad Bhagavata Purana Book X)*, Penguin Classics, 2004.

—*The Indo-Aryan Controversy: Evidence and Inference in Indian history*, Routledge, 2005.

Bulhof, Ilse N. and ten Kate, Laurens, eds., *Flight of the Gods: Philosophical Perspectives on Negative Theology*, Fordham Univ Press, 2000.

Campbell, June, *Traveller in Space: Gender, Identity and Tibetan Buddhism*, Continuum, London/NY, 2002.

*Cassell's New Latin Dictionary*, ed. D.P. Simpson, Funk & Wagnalls, NY 1960.

*The Catholic Encyclopedia*, XI, eds. Charles G. Herbermann, et al., The Encyclopedia Press, NY, 1913.

Chapman, Nathaniel, *Select Speeches, Forensick and Parliamentary*, IV, B.B. Hopkins and Co., Philadelphia, 1807.

*Charitonis Aphrodisiensis de Chaerea et Callirhoe amatoriarum narrationum libri octo*, ed. W.E. Blake, Clarendon Press, Oxford, 1938.

Collier, Mark and Manley, Bill, *How to Read Egyptian Hieroglyphs*, University of California Press, 2003.

Condell, Pat, "Free Speech is Sacred," www.youtube.com/watch?v=8bzTA_D5NpU

Cox, George, *Mythology of the Aryan Nations*, Longmans, 1870.

Crossan, John Dominic, *The Historical Jesus: The Life of a Mediterranean Jewish Peasant*, Harper, San Francisco, 1991.

Curran, John Philpot, *Speeches of John Philpot Curran*, Stockdale, Dublin, 1805.

Dasgupta, Punyapriya, *Cheated by the World: The Palestinian Experience*, Orient Longman, 1988.

Dawkins, Richard, *The God Delusion*, Houghton Mifflin Company, Boston/NY, 2006.

Dawood, N.J., tr., *The Koran*, Penguin Classics, 1990.
—*The Koran: With a Parallel Arabic Text*, Penguin Classics, 2006.

DeMeo, James, *Saharasia*, Natural Energy Works, OR, 1998, 2006.

De Troyer, Kristin, et al., *Wholly Woman, Holy Blood: A Feminist Critique of Purity and Impurity*, Trinity Press International, 2003.

Doane, T.W., *Bible Myths and Their Parallels in Other Religions*, Health Research, WA, 1985.

Draper, George Otis, *Searching for Truth*, Peter Eckler, London, 1902.

D'Souza, Dinesh, *What's So Great About Christianity?*, Regnery Publishing, 2007.

Eagle Nebula Image, ESA/Hubble, www.spacetelescope.org/images/html/opo9544a.html

Eastmond, Antony, *Art and Identity in Thirteenth-Century Byzantium*, Ashgate Publishing, 2004.

Eisenberg, Ronald L., *The JPS Guide to Jewish Traditions*, Jewish Publication Society of America, 2004.

Ellens, J. Harold, *Sex in the Bible: a New Consideration*, Greenwood Publishing Group, 2006.

Emerson, Ralph Waldo, *Representative Men: Nature, Addresses and Lectures*, Houghton Mifflin and Company, Boston/NY, 1883.

Evinger, James S., *Clergy Sexual Abuse: Annotated Bibliography of Conceptual and Practical Resources*, Rochester, NY, 2002; www.advocateweb.org/hope/pdf/evingerbiblio.pdf

Feder, Kenneth L., *Frauds, Myths and Mysteries: Science and Pseudoscience in Archaeology*, McGraw-Hill, Boston, 2008.

Ferguson, Everett, *Backgrounds of Early Christianity*, Wm. B. Eerdmans Publishing, 2003.

Finkelstein, Israel and Silberman, Neil Asher, *The Bible Unearthed: Archaeology's New Vision of Ancient Israel and the Origin of Its Sacred Texts*, The Free Press, 2001.

Finley, Mark, *The Next Superpower: Ancient Prophecies, Global Events, and Your Future*, Review & Herald Publishing, 2005.

Fontaine, Nicolas, *L'histoire du Vieux et du Nouveau Testament*, Chez P. Le Petit, Paris, 1686.

Frankel, Benjamin, *The Cold War, 1945-1991*, 2, Gale Research, 1992.

Frazer, James George, *The Golden Bough: A Study in Magic and Religion*, II, MacMillan and Co., London/NY, 1900.
—*The Golden Bough*, Collier, NY, 1963.
—*The Golden Bough: A New Abridgement*, Oxford University Press, 1998.

*Free Bible Illustrations*, www.freebibleillustrations.com

Freedman, David Noel, ed., *Eerdmans Dictionary of the Bible*, Wm. B. Eerdmans Publishing, 2000.

Giddens, Sandra and Giddens, Owens, *Chinese Mythology*, The Rosen Publishing Group, NY, 2006.

Glazov, Jamie, "The Infidel Revolution," www.frontpagemag.com/readArticle.aspx?ARTID=42

Graves, Kersey, *The Biography of Satan: Exposing the Origins of the Devil*, Book Tree, 1999.

Green, Tanya L., "Afghan Women Brutalized by the Taliban," www.cwfa.org/articles/1758/CWA/misc/index.htm, 10/29/2001.

Gross, Rita M., *Buddhism after Patriarchy: A Feminist History, Analysis, and Reconstruction of Buddhism*, SUNY Press, 1993.

Gutschow, Kim, *Being a Buddhist Nun: The Struggle for Enlightenment in the Himalayas*, Harvard University Press, 2004.

Halperin, David M., et al., *Before Sexuality: The Construction of Erotic Experience in the Ancient Greek World*, Princeton University Press, 1991.

Hanlon, Michael, "So is free will really just an illusion?", *UK Daily Mail Online*, www.dailymail.co.uk/sciencetech/article-560149/So-free-really-just-illusion.html

Harris, Ian, ed., *Buddhism and Politics in Twentieth-Century Asia*, Continuum, London/NY, 2001.

Haugen, Brenda, *Joseph Stalin: Dictator of the Soviet Union*, Compass Point Books, 2006.

Hawley, John Stratton, *Sati: The Blessing and The Curse*, Oxford University Press, 1994.

*The Herald of Gospel Liberty*, The Christian Publishing Association, OH, 1/5/1922.

Herodas, *The Mimes of Herodas*, ed. John Arbuthnot Nairn, Clarendon Press, Oxford, 1904.

Herodotus, *The Histories*, tr. Robin Waterfield, Oxford University Press, 1998.

Hervey, G. Winfred, *The Story of Baptist Missions in Foreign Lands*, Chancy R. Barns, St. Louis, 1884.

Hoet, Gerard, *Figures de la Bible*, Pieter de Hondt, 1728.

*Homeri Odyssea*, ed. P. von der Mühll, Helbing & Lichtenhahn, Basil, 1962.

Honour, Hugh and Fleming, John, *A World History of Art*, Laurence King, 2005.

Hopkins, John Henry, *A Candid Examination of the Question Whether the Pope of Rome is the Great Antichrist of Scripture*, Hurd and Houghton, NY, 1868.

Hornung, Erik, *The Valley of the Kings: Horizon of Eternity*, tr. David Warburton, Timken Publishers, NY, 1990.

Howland, Courtney W., *Religious Fundamentalisms and the Human Rights of Women*, Palgrave MacMillan, 1999.

Ingersoll, Robert G., *The Works of Robert G. Ingersoll*, IV, C.P. Farrell, NY, 1915.
—*The Works of Robert G. Ingersoll*, XI, The Dresden Publishing Co., NY, 1902.

Inman, Cecil Mark, *A Celebration of Life: A Prisoner of War's 54-year Journey Since the Korean War*, Xulon Press, 2006.

Isaac, Benjamin H., *The Invention of Racism in Classical Antiquity*, Princeton University Press, 2006.

Jackson, Nicky Ali, ed., *Encyclopedia of Domestic Violence*, Routledge, NY/London, 2007.

Jackson, Samuel Macauley, ed., *The New Schaff-Herzog Encyclopedia of Religious Knowledge*, X, Funk and Wagnalls Company, NY/London, 1911.

Jamieson, Robert, Fausset, A.R. and Brown, David, *A Commentary, Critical and Explanatory on the Old and New Testaments*, I, S.S. Scranton and Company, 1875.

Jenson, Phillip Peter, *Graded Holiness: A Key to the Priestly Conception of the World, Journal for the Study of the Old Testament*, Supplement Series 106, Sheffield, 1992.

Jones, Alfred, *Jones' Dictionary of Old Testament Proper Names*, Kregel Publications, 1990.

Joy, Eileen, "Writing, Race, and the English Nation," www.siue.edu/~ejoy/eng505syllabusFA07.htm

Kingsborough, Edward King, *Antiquities of Mexico*, 7 vols., Robert Havell, London, 1831.

Kinsley, David R., *Hindu Goddesses: Vision of the Divine Feminine in the Hindu Religious Tradition*, Motilal Banarsidass, 1998.

Knight, Richard Payne, *The Symbolical Language of Ancient Art and Mythology*, ed. Alexander Wilder, J.W. Houton, NY, 1876.

Kreeft, Peter, *Fundamentals of the Faith: Essays in Christian Apologetics*, Ignatius Press, 1988.

Kuenen, Abraham, *The Religion of Israel to the Fall of the Jewish State*, I, tr. Alfred Heath May, Williams and Norgate, London, 1882.

Lafaye, Jacques, *Quetzalcoatl and Guadalupe: The Formation of Mexican National Consciousness 1531-1813*, tr. Benjamin Keen, The University of Chicago Press, Chicago/London, 1987.

Laurie, Hugh, "House," en.wikiquote.org/wiki/House_(TV_series) —"Quotes on Religion," mindprod.com/religion/rquote.html

Layard, Austen H., *Discoveries Among the Ruins of Nineveh and Babylon*, Harper Brothers, NY, 1856.

Leedom, Tim C., ed., *The Book Your Church Doesn't Want You to Read*, The Truth Seeker Company, 1993.

Léon-Portilla, Miguel, ed., *Native Mesoamerican Spirituality*, Paulist Press, 1980.

Levy, Howard S., *Sex, Love and the Japanese*, Warm-Soft Village Press, 1971.

Lewis, Charlton T., *An Elementary Latin Dictionary*, American Book Company, Harper & Brothers, NY, 1890.

Lynn, Steven J. and Rhue, Judith W., eds., *Dissociation: Clinical and Theoretical Perspective*, Guilford Press, 1994.

Lyons, Eugene, *Stalin: Czar of All the Russians*, Deutsch Press, 2007.

Manuel, Frank E., *A Requiem for Karl Marx*, Harvard University Press, 1997.

Marcus, Jacob Rader, *United States Jewry, 1776-1985: The Germanic Period*, Wayne State University Press, 1992.

Martin, Michael, ed., *The Cambridge Companion to Atheism*, Cambridge University Press, 2007.

Marx/Engels Image Library, www.marxists.org/archive/marx/photo/

Maspero, Gaston, *The Struggle of the Nations: Egypt, Syria and Assyria*, ed. A.H. Sayce, Society for Promoting Christian Knowledge, London, 1896.

Massey, Gerald, *Ancient Egypt: The Light of the World*, I, T. Fisher Unwin, London, 1907.
—*Ancient Egypt: The Light of the World*, II, T. Fisher Unwin, London, 1907.

McKay, Alex, ed., *The History of Tibet: The Early Period to c. AD 850: The Yarlung Dynasty*, Routledge, 2003.

*The Merriam-Webster Dictionary*, 1994.

Miller, Calvin, *The Singer Trilogy: The Mythic Retelling of the New Testament*, InterVarsity Press, 1992.

Modrzejewski, Joseph Meleze, *The Jews of Egypt: From Ramses II to Emperor Hadrian*, Princeton University Press, 1997.

Monier-Williams, Monier, et al., *A Sanskrit-English Dictionary*, Motilal Banarsidass, 2005; www.srimadbhagavatam.org/downloads/Sanskrit Dictionary.html

Montefiore, Simon Sebag, *Stalin: The Court of the Red Tsar*, Random House, 2005.

Montgomery, Elizabeth, "Coverup: Behind the Iran-Contra Affair," Mpi Home Video, 2001.

Morley, John, *The Works of Voltaire*, VI, The Werner Company, OH, 1904.

Murdock, D.M., *Christ in Egypt: The Horus-Jesus Connection*, Stellar House Publishing, Seattle, 2009.

Muslim Women's League, www.mwlusa.org/topics/violence&harrassment/fgm.html

Nelson, Chris, "A Brief History of the Apocalypse," www.abhota.info/end1.htm

Nohrnberg, James, *Like unto Moses: The Constituting of an Interruption*, Indiana University Press, 1995.

Old Book Art, www.oldbookart.com/

Osho, *And the Flowers Showered*, Diamond Pocket Books, 1978.
—*The Divine Melody: Discourses on Songs of Kabir*, Diamond Pocket Books, 2003.
—*The Golden Wind*, vol. 1, July 1, 1980.

Patel, Tulsi, *Sex-Selective Abortion in India: Gender, Society and New Reproductive Technologies*, Sage Publications, 2001.

Patrick, Simon, *A Commentary upon the Two Books of Samuel*, Ri. Chiswell, London, 1703; openlibrary.org/details/commentaryupontw00patriala

Peggs, James, *India's Cries to British Humanity*, Simpkin and Marshall, London, 1832.

*The Pictorial Bible, being the Old and New Testaments*, I, Charles Knight & Co., London, 1836.

Pigault-Lebrun, *Le Citateur*, I, Gustave Barba, Paris, 1832.

Porter, Stanley E., *Hearing the Old Testament in the New Testament*, Wm. B. Eerdmans Publishing, 2006.

Purchas, Samuel, *Hakluytus Posthumus or Purchas His Pilgrimes*, XV, James MacLehose and Sons/The Macmillan Company, Glasgow/NY, 1906.

Radinsky, Edvard, *Stalin: The First In-Depth Biography Based on Explosive New Documents from Russia's Secret Archives*, Anchor Books, 1997.

*The Random House College Dictionary*, Random House, 1975.

Rankin, David Ivan, *From Clement to Origen: The Social and Historical Context of the Church Fathers*, Ashgate Publishing, Ltd., 2006.

Ravage, Maurice, "A Real Case Against the Jews," *The Century Magazine*, v. 115, no. 3, The Century Co., NY, 1927/1928.

Rawlinson, George, *The Five Great Monarchies of the Ancient Eastern World*, III, John Murray, London, 1865.

Reed, Christine F., et al., *Neighboring Faiths: Exploring Religions with Junior High Youth*, Unitarian Universalist, 1997.

Remsburg, John E., *The Christ: A Critical Review and Analysis of the Evidence of His Existence*, Prometheus Books, 1994.
—*Bible Morals*, Truth Seeker, NY, 1885.

Roberts, Alexander and Donaldson, James, eds., *The Ante-Nicene Fathers*, I, Charles Scribner's Sons, 1903.
—*The Ante-Nicene Fathers*, II, The Christian Literature Publishing Company, 1885.

Rockhill, W. Woodville, *The Life of the Buddha and the Early History of His Order*, Kegan Paul, 1907.

Rose, Carol, *Spirits, Fairies, Gnomes and Goblins: An Encyclopedia of the Little People*, ABC-CLIO, 1996.

Rosen, Steven J., *Essential Hinduism*, Greenwood Publishing Group, 2006.

Rossi, Paolo, *The Dark Abyss of Time: The History of the Earth and the History of Nations from Hooke to Vico*, tr. Lydia G. Cochrane, University of Chicago Press, 1987.

Russell, Bertrand, *Why I Am Not a Christian*, Simon & Schuster, 1957.

Russell, Jeffrey Burton, *The Devil: Perceptions of Evil from Antiquity to Primitive Christianity*, Cornell University Press, 1987.

Sagan, Carl, *U.S. News and World Report*, December 23, 1991.

Satyakama, Acharya, "The Need for Correct Understanding of Religion," groups.yahoo.com/group/superconsciousness/files/Acharya Satyakama/

Savage, Minot Judson, *The Religion of Evolution*, Lockwood, Brooks & Company, Boston, 1876.

Schechter, Harold and Everitt, David, *The A to Z Encyclopedia of Serial Killers*, Pocket Books, 2006.

Segal, Erich, ed., *The Dialogues of Plato*, Bantam Classics, 1986.

Sharpe, Samuel, *Egyptian Mythology and Egyptian Christianity*, J.R. Smith, London, 1863.

Siegel, Rachel Josefowitz and Cole, Ellen, ed., *Celebrating the Lives of Jewish Women: Patterns in a Feminist Sampler*, Routledge, 1997.

Silberstein, Laurence J. and Cohn, Robert L., ed., *The Other in Jewish Thought and History*, NYU Press, 1994.

Spencer, Robert, *Religion of Peace? Why Christianity Is and Islam Isn't*, Regnery Publishing, 2007.

Spicer, William Ambrose, *Our Day in the Light of Prophecy*, Kessinger, 1998.

Spurgeon, Caroline F.E., *Mysticism in English Literature*, BiblioBazaar, 2007.

Stone, Merlin, *When God was a Woman*, Barnes & Noble Publishing, 1990.

Strong, James, *The New Strong's Exhaustive Concordance of the Bible*, T. Nelson Publishers, 1990.

Taylor, Robert, *The Diegesis, being a Discovery or the Origin, Evidences, and Early History of Christianity*, Richard Carlile, London, 1829.

Taylor, Thomas, tr., *The Hymns of Orpheus*, BiblioBazaar, 2009.

Taxil, Leo, *Le Mystères de la Franc-Maçonnerie*, Paris, 1890.

Telushkin, Joseph, *Jewish Literacy: The Most Important Things to Know About the Jewish Religion, Its People, and Its History*, HarperCollins, 1991.

Thompson, Edward, *Suttee: A Historical and Philosophical Enquiry into the Hindu Rite of Widow-Burning*, George Allen & Unwin, London, 1928.

Titcomb, Sarah, *Aryan Suns Myths: The Origins of Religions*, Kessinger, 2005.

Vallely, Paul, "I was a Tantric sex slave," www.independent.co.uk/arts-entertainment/i-was-a-tantric-sex-slave-1069859.html

Voltaire, *A Philosophical Dictionary*, I, W. Dugdale, London, 1843.

Vossius, Gerardus Joannes, *De theologia gentili et physiologia Christiana, De origine et progressu idololatriae*, Sumptibus Casparis Waechtleri, 1641.

Walker, Barbara, *The Women's Encyclopedia of Myths and Secrets*, HarperCollins, NY, 1983.

Wasserfall, Rahel R., ed., *Women and Water: Menstruation in Jewish Life and Law*, Brandeis University Press, 1999.

Weinbrot, Howard D., *Eighteenth-Century Satire: Essays on Text and Context from Dryden to Peter Pindar*, Cambridge University Press, Cambridge, 2007.

Wheen, Francis, *Karl Marx: A Life*, W. W. Norton & Company, 2001.

Whiston, William, *The Works of Flavius Josephus*, II, J.B. Lippincott & Co., 1856.

Wikimedia Commons, commons.wikimedia.org/wiki/Main_Page

Zepa, tr., *An Eye-Opener, "Citateur, par Pigault." Le Brun, Doubts of Infidels*, William White and Company, Boston, 1871.

# Index

## Q

Quetzalcoatl, 106
Quran. *See* Koran, Quran

## R

Ra, 77
rabbis, 29, 34, 45, 130
Radinsky, Edvard, 130
*Ramayana*, 142
Ravage, Marcus Eli, 35
Rawlinson, George, 83, 84
Red Sea, 71, 72
Remsburg, John E., 33, 40, 111, 112
Revelation, 20, 89, 92, 93, 94, 95, 96
Rig Veda, 82, 84
Romans, Epistle to, 53, 55, 150
Rome, Romans, iv, vi, 100, 105, 125, 126
Rosen, Steven J., 70
Russell, Bertrand, 32
Russell, Jeffrey B., 79

## S

Sagan, Carl, 9
Sahagun, 108
saints, 35, 61, 82
salvation, 67, 155
Samaria, Samaritans, 103, 104
Samuel, First Book of, 73, 112, 114
Samuel, prophet, 101
Samuel, Second Book of, 109, 112, 113
Sanskrit, 70, 82, 83, 84, 85, 143

Sarah, 70, 111
Sarasvati, 70
Satan, 11, 22, 56, 77, 79, 80, 86
Satanism, 118
*sati, suttee*, 141, 142, 143
Satyakama, Acharya, 1
scapegoat, 54, 55, 99
Schechter, Harold, 115
Schwartz, 23
scripture, 38, 90, 105, 150, 163, 164, 166, 167
secret societies, 93
serpent, 56, 71, 97
Serpent of the Underworld, 76, 78
Set, Seth, 74, 75, 77
Seti, 77
sex, 14, 55, 110, 111, 134, 141, 144, 161
sexism, 26, 56, 140, 145, 146, 156
Sharpe, Samuel, 94
*sheitel*, 139
Shu, 75
Singer, Margaret T., 25, 118, 126
sinister, 76, 123
skeptics, 47
slavery, 151, 169
Solomon, 112
*songyums*, 141
South Pole, 74
Spain, Spanish, 83, 104, 107
Spurgeon, Caroline F.E., 66
Stalin, Josef, 130
Star Trek, 14
stars, 6, 75, 81, 97
Stone Age, 7, 23
Sumerians, 69

D.M. Murdock, also known as "Acharya S," studied Classics, Greek Civilization, at Franklin & Marshall College in Lancaster, PA. She is also an alumna of the American School of Classical Studies at Athens, Greece. Ms. Murdock is the author of the controversial books *The Christ Conspiracy: The Greatest Story Ever Sold*; *Suns of God: Krishna, Buddha and Christ Unveiled*; *Who Was Jesus? Fingerprints of The Christ*; and *Christ in Egypt: The Horus-Jesus Connection*. Murdock has been online since 1995, and many of her articles on the subjects of comparative religion, mythology and astrotheology can be found on her websites TruthBeKnown.com, StellarHousepublishing.com, TBKNews.blogspot.com and FreethoughtNation.com.

Don't Miss these Great Books from—

# Stellar House Publishing

***Christ in Egypt:***
***The Horus-Jesus Connection***
by D.M. Murdock/Acharya S

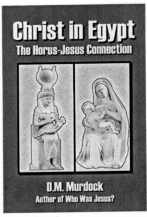

Destined to be a classic enjoyed by both the professional scholar and the layperson, this comparative religion book contains a startling perspective of the extraordinary history of the Egyptian religion and its profound influence upon the later Christian faith. *Christ in Egypt*: *The Horus-Jesus Connection* uses a massive amount of primary sources and the works of highly credentialed authorities in relevant fields to demonstrate that the popular gods Horus and Jesus possessed many characteristics and attributes in common.

Drawing from thousands of ancient Egyptian texts in an assortment of translations along with the original language, as well as modern research in a number of other languages, controversial independent scholar D.M. Murdock puts together an astonishing amount of fascinating information that shows many of our most cherished religious beliefs did not appear suddenly out of the blue but have long histories in numerous cultures found around the globe, including and especially in the glorious Land of the Pharaohs.

6 x 9 | 574 pages | ISBN-13: 978-0979963117 | $26.95

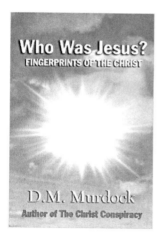

**Who Was Jesus?**
**Fingerprints of The Christ**
by D.M. Murdock/Acharya S

Was Jesus Christ truly the divine Son of God who walked the earth 2,000 years ago? How can we be sure the gospel story is an accurate and infallibly related historical account? When the gospels are examined scientifically, can we truthfully uphold them as "inerrant?"

Is it possible to assert honestly and ethically that the Bible is the inspired Word of God? The answers to these questions and many more may surprise and shock you!

Is the New Testament a "historical record" or "factual biography" of what really happened, or a tool for the priesthood to lay down doctrines and dogma as they were developed over the centuries?

5.5 x 8.5 | 284 pages | ISBN-13: 978-979963100 | $17.95

www.StellarHousePublishing.com

LaVergne, TN USA
10 November 2010
204271LV00001B/36/P